SpringerBriefs in Political Science

SpringerBriefs present concise summaries of cutting-edge research and practical applications across a wide spectrum of fields. Featuring compact volumes of 50 to 125 pages, the series covers a range of content from professional to academic. Typical topics might include:

- A timely report of state-of-the art analytical techniques
- A bridge between new research results, as published in journal articles, and a contextual literature review
- A snapshot of a hot or emerging topic
- An in-depth case study or clinical example
- A presentation of core concepts that students must understand in order to make independent contributions

SpringerBriefs in Political Science showcase emerging theory, empirical research, and practical application in political science, policy studies, political economy, public administration, political philosophy, international relations, and related fields, from a global author community.

SpringerBriefs are characterized by fast, global electronic dissemination, standard publishing contracts, standardized manuscript preparation and formatting guidelines, and expedited production schedules.

Giovanna Maria Dora Dore •
Arya D. McCarthy • James A. Scharf

A Free Press, If You Can Keep It

What Natural Language Processing Reveals About Freedom of the Press in Hong Kong

Springer

Giovanna Maria Dora Dore
East Asia Studies Program, Krieger School of Arts and Sciences
Johns Hopkins University
Baltimore, MD, USA

Arya D. McCarthy
Center for Language and Speech Processing, Whiting School of Engineering
Johns Hopkins University
Baltimore, MD, USA

James A. Scharf
Applied Physics Laboratory
Johns Hopkins University
Baltimore, MD, USA

ISSN 2191-5466 ISSN 2191-5474 (electronic)
SpringerBriefs in Political Science
ISBN 978-3-031-27583-8 ISBN 978-3-031-27584-5 (eBook)
https://doi.org/10.1007/978-3-031-27584-5

This Springer imprint is published by the registered company Springer Nature Switzerland AG
The registered company address is: Gewerbestrasse 11, 6330 Cham, Switzerland

Acknowledgments

This book presents the key findings emerging from the *Media Portraits of Protests in Hong Kong Project*, which combines natural language processing with qualitative investigation of patterns of journalistic practice across selected Hong Kong- and western-based newspapers to investigate changes in press freedom in Hong Kong between 1998 and 2020. To the extent that we succeeded, we would like to recognize scholars and colleagues who have helped along the way.

We are indebted to Tom Lippincott for his advice and guidance in identifying new modeling techniques. Karl D. Jackson and David Lazer for their suggestions on how the *Media Portraits of Protests in Hong Kong Project* could create opportunities for collaborations between computational science and social science. Francis Lee for his advice on data sources on survey-based citizens' attitudes towards the Hong Kong press. Lucy Li for her suggestions on natural language processing background materials relevant for our manuscript. Special thanks to Julia Colen and Trenton Wang for their help at the outset of the project implementation, and Mickey McCarthy for providing lexical insights and editorial suggestions on earlier versions of the manuscript.

We would like to acknowledge the Krieger School of Arts and Sciences and the Whiting School of Engineering of the Johns Hopkins University for providing an intellectually stimulating environment that has allowed the *Media Portraits of Protests in Hong Kong Project* to flourish and deliver results that will further interdisciplinary growth and insight. We are grateful to the 4th Workshop on Challenges and Application of Automated Extraction of Socio-political Events from Text (CASE), the 4th and 5th Annual Politics and Computational Social Science Conference (PaCSS), the 6th SIGHUM Workshop on Computational Linguistics for Cultural Heritage, Social Science, Humanities and Literature (LaTeCH), the 11th and 12th Annual Conference on New Directions in Analyzing Text as Data (TADA), the 79th Annual Midwest Political Science Conference (MPSA), the 13th Language Resources and Evaluation Conference (LREC), and the outreach activities under our APSA Centennial Grant *Learning How to Play with Machines* for providing opportunities to present and receive feedback on the findings emerging from the *Media Portraits of Protests in Hong Kong Project*. These opportunities allowed us to test the validity of our pioneering methodology, refine the presentation, and broaden the reach of our research findings.

Jamie A. Scharf would like to thank his advisors for their guidance which helped him grow as a researcher, programmer, and social scientist. He also thanks his friends and family for encouraging him to combine his interests in language, computing, and politics. Finally, he dedicates this book to his grandparents, who have been the perfect role models for life-long learning and laughing.

Arya D. McCarthy would like to express his gratitude to his mother and grandmother for their unwavering and inspirational nature as role models over decades. Several friends have shown excess kindness toward him, especially in recent months. Their support has given him the comfort and clarity to continue his work, for which words cannot convey his thanks. He further thanks the Center for Language and Speech Processing for fostering a rich intellectual environment to discuss the confluence of language and statistics.

Giovanna Maria Dora Dore is grateful for her family and friends tolerating her incessant book drafting disappearances over the last several months. Giovanna would also like to thank Arya and Jamie for generously sharing their knowledge and experience about computational linguistics, and her mentors' never-failing encouragement for her to push the boundaries of social inquiry. She dedicates this book to her niece Carlotta.

Contents

Chapter 1
Introduction

This is an interdisciplinary book. In it we introduce mixed-methods research approaches to a social-scientific inquiry about the freedom of the press in Hong Kong. Specifically, we pair computational analyses from the field of natural language processing with qualitative analysis of patterns of journalistic practice in volatile political settings. Together, these shed light on the evolution of press freedom since the return of Hong Kong to Chinese sovereignty. Although Article 27 of the Basic Law– Hong Kong's Constitution– acknowledges the right to freedom of the press and expression,[1] press freedom is not unequivocally protected in Hong Kong (Foster, 1998). In fact, the National People's Congress of China holds the right to interpret the Basic Law and other laws that could limit press freedom. Beyond this, Beijing can also influence the Hong Kong media by *co-opting media owners* (Lee, 2007), setting *norms of journalistic political correctness* (Lau & To, 2002), and employing *strategic ambiguity* (Cheung, 2003) to induce *self-censorship* (Lee et al., 2006). The interplay of these tactics may induce *shifts in journalistic paradigms* (Chan & Lee, 1984) and, over time, result in a subtle erosion of press freedom.

To assess changes in press freedom, we focus on the volatile topic of protests and their news coverage. Protests constitute an important means in contemporary societies through which citizens voice their concerns and exercise their right to free speech. Most protests, however, happen at specific times and places, and are witnessed by relatively small numbers of people. As such, their success is predicated on whether and how mass media, and especially newspapers, portray them (Agnone, 2007; King, 2011). While "there is no formula to determine whether something is newsworthy" (Lorenz & Vivian, 1996: 22), there is agreement that features such as "unusual, timely, local or nearby, surprising, about change, conflict and people, has impact, evokes human interest, and conveys information" (Cotter, 2010: 68) make

[1] https://www.basiclaw.gov.hk/en/basiclaw/chapter3.html

G. M. D. Dore et al., *A Free Press, If You Can Keep It*, SpringerBriefs in Political Science,
https://doi.org/10.1007/978-3-031-27584-5_1

events valuable to the press. Protests are a natural fit to these parameters, so they are inherently newsworthy (Liebes & Blum-Kulka, 2004) which, in turn, makes newspapers invaluable for protest events (Earl et al., 2004).

News coverage, however, can be a double-edged sword. Newspapers can either amplify and legitimize the protesters' voices, thus enhancing the chances for protests to enlist public support and influence authorities (Gamson & Wolfsfeld, 1993), or marginalize and delegitimize protests through portraying them as perilous or irrelevant (Boykoff, 2006). Recognizing that the relationship between newspapers and protests is a dynamic one, and that "dissonance across media outlets could be socially and politically consequential" (Tsfati & Walter, 2019: 39), our analysis of press freedom is grounded in an account of the occurrence and evolution of protests in Hong Kong between 1998 and 2020.

Protest participation has long been an undercurrent in Hong Kong's political culture, even though large-scale demonstrations have become more prominent in the post-handover era. On July 1, 1997, Beijing regained sovereignty over Hong Kong, and on July 2, 1997, thousands of people marched the streets of Hong Kong, in the rain, demanding democracy. Since then, the anniversary of the handover has been marked by both official celebrations and street processions, with varied citizens' turnout depending on the social and political issues gripping Hong Kong. In 2003, the July 1 march registered the participation of 500,000 citizens clad in black who protested the proposed National Security Law, and forced the government to postpone its discussion in the Legislative Council (LegCo)[2] (Lawrence & Martin, 2020). The proposed security law was not as draconian as the British colonial regulations it intended to replace—imposed following anti-British riots in the 1920s and 1960s[3] and rarely invoked. Yet, its most controversial provision would have allowed the Hong Kong government to ban any group with links to an organization that had been banned by Beijing in the rest of China for national security reasons. This July first protest was the largest in Hong Kong since 1989, when Hongkongers marched to protest the Tiananmen Square incidents, the largest protest ever directed against the Hong Kong government itself, and the largest anywhere on Chinese soil since the occupation of Tiananmen Square. The July 1 protest altered the political dynamics in Hong Kong, led to the formation of new political groups, and strengthened citizens' civic assertiveness (Cheng, 2016).

As protests and rallies became more frequent, with participation ranging anywhere from tens of thousands to millions (Chan & Lee, 2007), they also started to lose their power, which created incentives for protests' escalation and radicalization

[2] The Legislative Council is Hong Kong's legislature and comprises 70 members, 35 of whom are directly elected by five geographical constituencies under proportional representation. The remaining 35 members are indirectly elected through interest group–based functional constituencies, with limited electorates. Since its establishment in 1843, as an advisory council to the Governor, the powers and functions of the Legislative Council have expanded. https://www.legco.gov.hk/general/english/members/

[3] https://www.scmp.com/magazines/post-magazine/long-reads/article/2089195/witnesses-anarchy-1967-riots-hong-kong-some-those

(Cheng, 2014). The 2006 Star and Queen protest against the demolition of the Edinburgh Place Ferry Pier and the Queen's Pier, "two humble structures that had served cross-harbor transportation at the city's financial district for nearly half a century" (Ting, 2013: 80), lasted for ninety-seven days. Its tenacity, "remarkable political vibrancy and cultural ingenuity" (Ting, 2013: 83) turned the piers into symbols of collective identity and political contestation of urban development. In 2012, the Scholarism movement[4] brought together secondary school students and teachers to defend the autonomy of education and oppose lawmakers' attempt to impose a Moral and National Education curriculum (M&NEC) to Hong Kong. A parade of 90,000 people was held at the end of July. Then, at the end of August, members from Scholarism staged a hunger strike and *Occupy Civic Square* by setting up a stage in the forecourt of the government headquarters. On 1 September—the first day of a new semester—protesters held a carnival-demonstration, after which the thousands of participants joined *Occupy Civic Square*, turning the space into a venue for public discussion about the M&NEC. The government suspended M&NEC on September 8 and abandoned the proposal completely on September 11, following the Hong Kong Federation of Students' half-day class boycott. The anti-M&NEC protests' success highlighted the relevance of youth interest groups in shaping policymaking through direct action.

It was, however, the 2014 Occupy Central protests[5] that caught the attention of the press both in Hong Kong and abroad. The Chinese government had promised that the 2017 election of the chief executive would be by universal suffrage. However, on June 10, 2014, to make sure that no subversive politician would be elected as chief executive, Beijing issued a white paper on the principle of *one country, two systems,*[6] stating that "the high degree of autonomy of the Hong Kong-SAR is not full autonomy, nor a decentralized power (…) subject to central leadership's authorization."[7] Then, on August 31, Beijing announced a new electoral framework for Hong Kong, in which candidates would need to obtain support from more than half of the nomination committee's 1200 members to stand in the election. As China was likely to control the nomination committee, the new electoral framework would

[4] https://socialmovements.trinity.duke.edu/groups/scholarism

[5] https://www.reuters.com/article/us-hongkong-politics-occupy-explainer/explainer-what-was-hong-kongs-occupy-movement-all-about-idUSKCN1S005M

[6] "The idea of *one country, two systems* originated in 1979, when China offered to allow Taiwan to keep its economic and social systems, government, and even military in return for acknowledging that it was part of the People's Republic. Taiwan rejected that proposal. [Then-Premier] Deng Xiaoping next used the idea to resolve an emergent crisis over Hong Kong. The biggest section of Hong Kong, the New Territories, was scheduled to revert to mainland rule in 1997, and real-estate investors feared they would lose everything in the reversion. Those concerns led to a historic confrontation between Deng and [British Prime Minister] Margaret Thatcher in December 1984, and the Sino-British Joint Declaration of 1984, which promised "to preserve the judicial system, legislative and executive autonomy, and all the key freedoms to which Hong Kong people had become accustomed for 50 years." Overholt, W. (2019). *Hong Kong: The Rise and Fall of "One Country, Two Systems,* Boston: Harvard Kennedy School, p. 1.

[7] http://english.www.gov.cn/archive/white_paper/2014/08/23/content_281474982986578.htm

allow ruling out *problematic* candidates. Hongkongers responded to the announcement of the new electoral framework with Occupy Central.[8] While intended as a peaceful, disobedience campaign to force the Chinese government to grant universal suffrage to Hong Kong, it turned into the Umbrella Movement[9] and a 79-day intermittent occupation of downtown Hong Kong—from September 28th to December 15th of 2014. Occupy Central and the Umbrella Movement did not succeed in bringing universal suffrage to Hong Kong, and yet they became the worldwide symbol of Hongkongers' action against Beijing "chipping away at Hong Kong's freedoms."[10]

Protest radicalization continued to grow in 2016, a year punctuated by multiple episodes of civic unrest to counter what Hongkongers perceived as Beijing growing unease with their calls for democracy and autonomy. Some of most heated protests erupted over a new election procedure requiring candidates running for the LegCo's elections to sign a form *acknowledging Hong Kong as an inseparable part of China*.[11] It was, however, the 2019–2020 protests against the amendment to the Fugitive Offenders and Mutual Legal Assistance in Criminal Matters Legislation Bill (ELAB)[12] that set new highs for protests' violence and radicalization. Opponents to ELAB argued that the proposed amendment would weaken the *one country, two systems*[13] provisions for Hong Kong's judiciary to remain independent and "effectively remove the legal firewall between the city and the mainland" (Ibrahim & Lam, 2020: 54). Early demonstrations to voice dissent morphed into an increasingly forceful anti-government, anti-Beijing movement, with demands for greater democracy and police accountability. Hong Kong citizens' militancy captured domestic and international media attention. The news value of the protests increased as they became the largest in Hong Kong's history—and the largest to date on Chinese soil—and their objectives shifted from protesting the extradition bill to protecting democracy.

To investigate changes in press freedom in Hong Kong post-1997, we rely on the *Hong Kong Protest News Dataset* (©DoreGMD), a curated collection of 4522 news articles covering protests that took place in Hong Kong between 1998 and 2020. News sources contributing to the dataset include two Hong Kong–based, English

[8] Often compared to Wall Street, the Central district is Hong Kong's financial and business center, and where the headquarters of major international and domestic corporations and numerous countries' consulates are located. https://www.scmp.com/article/1604649/what-occupy-central-10-things-you-need-know

[9] The name Umbrella Movement comes from the protesters' use of umbrellas to shield themselves from tear gas and pepper spray that the police used to disperse protesters.

[10] Lindsay Maizland and Eleanor Albert. 2021. "Hong Kong's Freedoms: What China Promised and How It's Cracking Down." *Council of Foreign Relations*, 100 |Backgrounders. https://www.cfr.org/backgrounder/hong-kong-freedoms-democracy-protests-china-crackdown

[11] https://carnegieendowment.org/2016/10/17/implications-of-sixth-hong-kong-legislative-election-for-relations-with-beijing-pub-64872

[12] https://www.legco.gov.hk/yr18-19/english/bills/b201903291.pdf

[13] See footnote no. 6

language newspapers: the *China Daily* and the *South China Morning Post*; and six western-based, English language newspapers: *The New York Times*, *The Wall Street Journal*, *The Washington Post*, *The Financial Times*, *The Guardian*, and *The Times*. Current limitations of comparison across languages made the challenge of including news sources in Cantonese and Mandarin formidable and ultimately resulted in the decision to include only English language newspapers (Du et al., 2018). The scope and scale of our corpus makes it amenable to diachronic and synchronic analysis, testing the robustness of changes in newspapers' treatment of protests over time. It also sharply contrasts previous corpora focused on protest in Hong Kong, the largest of which has 40% as many articles spanning half as many years.

To meet the challenges inherent in operationalizing our research we used a mixed-method approach that combines natural language processing (NLP) with a qualitative investigation of patterns of journalistic practice across newspapers. This powerful combination builds on existing application-based validation efforts, and the ongoing debate on the operational implications of computational procedures (Baden et al. 2021). As language is at the heart of our research, NLP emerges as especially important for its ability "to analyze signals ranging from simple lexical clues to word clusters to choices of syntactic structure" (Boydstun et al., 2013: 2) as well as its speed, scale, granularity, and reliability when analyzing text.

Our analysis enlists several NLP techniques to investigate changes in press freedom in Hong Kong. *Topic modeling* contrasts the treatment of protests in Hong Kong diachronically and across news sources. *Comparison of lexical frequency* and *lexical usage* reveals preferences and discrepancies in the use of protest-relevant keywords in the newspapers' articles. *Computational sentiment analysis* measures the tone and connotations of articles and their headlines. *Embedding neighborhood comparisons* strengthen our understanding of how words are used differently between western- and Hong Kong-based newspapers, and also how the context of protest-related keywords may differ across news sources over time. Finally, *Granger causality* investigates whether protest news coverage impacts protests' size, which ultimately broadens our knowledge of access to free speech in Hong Kong.

Moreover, we pioneered a novel technique to connect lexically driven topic models (e.g., those created with MALLET or "stm") to deep, semantically driven topic models (e.g., those drawn from deep language models paired with robust clustering methods) to explore the variation in a corpus by combining signals from two perspectives, much akin to the merit of classifier combination or co-training (Blum & Mitchell, 1998). However, unlike the aforementioned procedures, ours uses the two signals in an unsupervised, exploratory way. We named this innovative approach *Vicinato Plots* (McCarthy 2021: A. Supplement: Vicinato Plots).

In the broader context of investigating press freedom in Hong Kong, the contributions that this book makes are manifold and, for ease of discussion, can be grouped as addressing the *non-rhetorical* and *rhetorical* techniques of the Hong Kong press.

Contributions analyzing *non-rhetorical* techniques include:

- *A mixed-method approach to govern our data analysis*. Our methodological choice broadens the application of NLP techniques to the social sciences without diluting conceptual standards or privileging the study of phenomena that are easily measurable (Baden et al., 2021). In its choice of methodology, the book helps close the gap between "social scientific, validity-focused methodological debates, and the prevalent mode of technologically driven computational text analysis methods development." (Baden et al., 2021: 13).
- *The Hong Kong Protest News Dataset*. We constructed a curated collection of 4522 news articles covering episodes of protests between 1998 and 2020. News sources contributing to the dataset include two Hong Kong–based, English language newspapers: the *China Daily* and the *South China Morning Post*, and six western-based, English language newspapers: *The New York Times*, *The Wall Street Journal*, *The Washington Post*, *The Financial Times*, *The Guardian*, and *The Times*. The scope and scale of our corpus makes it amenable to diachronic and synchronic analysis, testing the robustness of changes in newspapers' treatment of protests over time.
- *A contextualized understanding of the volume and timing or articles published.* Between 1998 and 2020, the SCMP and the China Daily published more articles about protests in Hong Kong than western-based newspapers—3728 vs. 794—except for 2014 when this trend was reversed—131 vs. 236. Hong Kong-based newspapers' coverage is consistent and sustained over time, whereas that of western-based newspapers is punctuated by sharps peaks and dips, and declines over time, most significantly between 2015–2020. The SCMP and China Daily published 4.7 times more articles than the NYT, WSJ, WaPo, FT, the Guardian, and the Times of London combined (i.e., 3728 vs. 794), with the SCMP publishing more than any other newspapers in the dataset. With 425 articles, the NYT published more than half of what all western-based newspapers in our dataset published on Hong Kong protests. These differences in the volume and timing of protests' coverage created an opportunity for the SCMP and the China Daily to set the agenda for how Hong Kong protests were framed and reported.
- *Granger causality investigation of news coverage on protests' size*. We found correlations between news coverage of protests and protests' size in the 2019–2020 anti-ELAB protests. We paired this finding with a qualitative review of the articles published in the SCMP, China Daily, and western-based newspapers and established that the Hong Kong-based newspapers played a *facilitator*, rather than a *mobilizer* role vis-à-vis the protests, as their main interest in covering the protests rested entirely on their news value rather than the reasons behind them.

Contributions analyzing *Rhetorical* techniques include:

- *The Vicinato plots*. The pioneering approach described on the previous page, combining lexically driven topic models to deep semantically driven ones, is given a proof of concept. The development of the Vicinato plots approach and its pilot application to the *Hong Kong Protest News Dataset* enriches NLP's analytical techniques in the field of topic modeling, and it furthers research straddling fields as diverse as comparative politics and computer science.

- *Diachronic consistency in how Hong Kong-based newspapers frame their coverage of protests*. Findings reveal that the SCMP and the China Daily consistently relied on six frames to portray protests in Hong Kong. This is an important and counterintuitive finding in light of the dynamisms of the protests as well as how they have evolved over time. We also found consistency between the frames that the SCMP and the China Daily used and those included in the Policy Frames Codebook (Boydstun et al., 2013: 4–5). This consistency strengthens the generalizability of our results on the characterization of protests beyond Hong Kong.
- *Systematic use of the protest paradigm to portray the Hong Kong protests.* Our data show that the China Daily and the SCMP methodically apply the *protest paradigm* when covering episodes of protest in Hong Kong, with a heightened emphasis on the disruptiveness and ineffectiveness of both the protests and protesters. Our analysis shows that western-based newspapers also rely on the protest paradigm in their coverage of the Hong Kong protests, yet they do so to characterize the protests "as a pro-democracy revolution, as a fight for freedom and pluralism, and the use of radical tactics and violence as the most effective means for protesters to be heard" (McCluskey et al., 2009: 361). This finding complements what the Granger causality analysis reveals and suggests that, opposite to the China Daily and the SCMP, western-based newspapers played both the role of *facilitator* and *mobilizer* vis-à-vis the protests, as they agreed both with the reasons why the protests were held and the radical tactics employed.
- *Stylometric differences across news sources reveal a significant negative tone in the Hong Kong–based newspapers' coverage of the protests, avoidance of discussing the reasons for the protests, and a preference for offering description of the events.* The SCMP emerged as the newspaper with the most negative tone in the coverage of the protests, and both the China Daily and SCMP used the terms *democracy* and *freedom* as qualifiers rather than as nouns. These rhetorical choices may be attributable to the type of articles that these newspapers publish. Across the large number of articles published, the SCMP and the China Daily focus relentlessly on the details of protests, an editorial choice that lends itself to using the terms *democracy* and *freedom* sparingly and as qualifiers and avoids discussing the values that the terms *democracy* and *freedom* embody vis a vis the protests.
- *An understanding of how Hong Kong-based newspapers use protest-related words.* The investigation of word embedding neighborhoods showcased the differences in how protest-related keywords are used across news sources, and of how the contexts of protest-related keywords differ across news sources over time. We confirmed semantic divergence in certain keywords both between Hong Kong– and western-based newspapers vis-à-vis particular episodes of protests. Between 1998 and 2020, the most significant semantic divergence is found in the lexical usage of the words *riot*, *protests*, *occupation*, and *confrontation*. Moreover, we found that the SCMP and the China Daily systematically relate the terms nearest neighbors to adversarial or hostile behavior, and use nouns in their singu-

lar form, which may signal the intention to criticize the values embodied in those nouns while reporting about them as objects or actions.

- *Differences-in-differences in how Hong Kong–based newspapers report on protests over time*. Using the 2019–2020 anti-ELAB protests as a case study, we confirmed that in the SCMP and the China Daily the semantic context of the protest keywords became more polarizing, compared with what happened in western-based newspapers. Our analysis also shows that June 2019 was a pivotal moment, after which the meaning of several keywords shifts for at least the remainder of 2019. In fact, in the first half of 2019, neighbors for *riots* include terms like *actions*, *open*, *engage*, and *taken* which are not charged and, in the context of either a reporting or an opinion piece, descriptively inform readers. However, in the second half of 2019, the nature of the neighboring terms for *riots* changes to include more polarizing terms such as *violent*, *escalated*, *destructive*, *triggered*, *anti-government*, and *sparked*.

Unfolding throughout the chapters of the book, the analysis of how newspapers portray protests sheds light on how press freedom has changed in Hong Kong in the post-handover years. In its choice of methodology, this book broadens the application of NLP techniques to the social sciences (Baden et al., 2021). In its choice of topic, the book fills a gap in the literature on Hong Kong printed media, particularly in relation to the political and social consequences of dissonance across media outlets in volatile political settings (Chan & Lee, 1984; Lee, 2014; Tsfati & Walter, 2019).

Chapter 2
Methodological Approach and Data

2.1 Methodological Approach

To meet the challenges inherent to operationalizing our research, we choose a mixed-methods approach which combines NLP with a qualitative investigation of patterns of journalistic practice across newspapers. As language is at the heart of our research, NLP emerges as especially important for its ability "to analyze signals ranging from simple lexical clues to word clusters to choices of syntactic structure" (Boydstun et al., 2013: 2). This, together with other NLP advantages to analyzing text, including speed, scale, consistency, reliability, and granularity, helps shed light on changes in press freedom by strengthening the current understanding of whether depth and/or manner of reporting changed over time, and if so, in what ways or in response to what.

When analyzing our data, we privileged the following NLP techniques:

- *Topic modeling* to contrast the treatment of protests in Hong Kong both diachronically and across news sources.
- *Comparison of lexical frequency* and *lexical usage* to reveal preferences and discrepancies in the use of protest-relevant keywords in the newspapers' articles.
- *Computational sentiment analysis* to measure the tone and connotations of articles and headlines.
- *Embedding neighborhood comparisons* to further understand how words are used differently between western- and Hong Kong-based newspapers, and also how the context of protest-related keywords may differ across news sources over time.
- *Granger causality testing* to investigate whether protest news coverage impacts the size of protests in Hong Kong.
- An innovative approach to connect lexically driven topic models (e.g., those created with MALLET or "stm") to deep, semantically driven topic models (e.g., those drawn from deep language models paired with robust clustering methods)

G. M. D. Dore et al., *A Free Press, If You Can Keep It*, SpringerBriefs in Political Science,
https://doi.org/10.1007/978-3-031-27584-5_2

to explore the variation in a corpus by combining signals from two perspectives, much akin to the merit of classifier combination or co-training (Blum & Mitchell, 1998). However, unlike the aforementioned approaches, our approach uses the two signals in an unsupervised, exploratory way. We named this innovative approach *Vicinato Plots* (McCarthy 2021: A. Supplement: Vicinato Plots).

In using statistical techniques from NLP, our book builds on Wueest et al. (2013), who apply topic models and named entity recognition to protest event analysis, and Hürriyetoğlu et al. (2019) who show that, computationally speaking, not all protests are alike as event extraction models for protests perform much worse on countries outside the training set. Inverting this, the research informing this book calls into question different views on protests in the same location. The research informing this book also benefits from earlier the work of Lucy et al. (2020) on the use of word embedding similarity, topic models, and dependency parsing to generate clues toward differing portrayals of race and gender in US history textbooks; Field et al. (2018), who relate the content of Russian state-run news articles to the nation's economic performance, finding an agenda of distraction; Mosteller and Wallace (1984) and Bergsma et al. (2012) on content analysis and stylometry in consideration of authorship; Koppel et al. (2005) on native language identification; Bednarek et al. (2021) on word frequency and collocation for identifying news values, and Ott et al. (2013) on deceptive product reviews.

Of further relevance to our research are Jatowt and Duh (2014) and Kulkarni et al. (2015) in relation to the detection of shifts in word meaning, whether between groups or over time, and gradual or at specific change points. Wijaya and Yeniterzi (2011), who show that relevant historical events lead to differences in word usage; Mihalcea (2012) who highlights approaches that rely on embedding words in a vector space, based on each word's usage and sentential context. Rudolph and Blei (2018) and Hofmann et al. (2021) who discuss how word vectors may be fitted with the temporal or social context in mind, whereas Hamilton et al. (2016) show how separate embedding spaces for each group may be aligned post hoc. Soni et al. (2021) use these embedding shift techniques on eleven nineteenth-century US newspapers to identify that "a multiracial coalition of women led the abolitionist movement in terms of both thought and action" (2021: 4). Finally, Blei and Lafferty's work (2006, 2007) which tracks shifts in entire topics, rather than in the semantics of individual words.

In terms of qualitative analysis, we employ qualitative content analysis (Lee, 2014; Fulcher, 2010) on a random sample of 30% of the article corpus (i.e., 1357 articles) to corroborate the results emerging from the application of NLP techniques. Our choice to use qualitative analysis to complement NLP techniques builds on the foundational Achen and Snidal's (1989) recommendation to use historical case studies as a complement to statistical research, Verba's work in the 1990s (Verba et al., 1993, 1995; Verba, 1996) and Tarrow's call for bridging qualitative and quantitative modes of research in social science (1995). More recently, the scholarship of Nguyen et al. (2015), Card et al. (2016), and Ylä-Anttila et al. (2020) helped showcase further the challenges and opportunities of research that integrates computational and qualitative text analyses. In our content analysis, we performed *decontextualization* to familiarize ourselves with the data; this step requires reading through the text to get a sense of the content. Then, selected the level of granularity relevant to the inquiry (Catanzaro, 1988; Graneheim & Lundman, 2004), with individual articles representing the meaning unit of our research for our corpus. Through *recontextualization*, we checked whether the content of the articles is pertinent to the topic (i.e., protests held in Hong Kong between 1998 and 2020) driving the research question (Burnard 1991). Finally, we perform *categorization*. The qualitative analysis of the articles' content was performed manually. While pre-identified categories initially guided the study, we expected others to emerge throughout the course of the analysis (Altheide & Schneider, 2013; Berg, 2007; Roberts & Pettigrew, 2007). As such, when the quantitative findings suggested additional categories (such as whether discuss the duty of police to maintain order), these were incorporated into the qualitative investigation. The results were cross-checked between four independent annotators, and only analyses with high inter-annotator agreement were retained.

In its choice of methodology, this book broadens the application of NLP techniques to the social sciences "without diluting conceptual standards or privileging the study of phenomena that are easily measurable" (Baden et al., 2021: 2). In doing so, our book helps narrow the gap between "social scientific, validity-focused methodological debates, and the prevalent mode of technologically driven computational text analysis methods development" (Baden et al., 2021: 13). In its findings, this book fills a gap in the literature on Hong Kong media, particularly in relation to the political and social consequences of dissonance across media outlets in volatile political settings (Lee, 2014; Tsfati & Walter, 2019).

2.2 The Hong Kong Protest News Dataset

The article corpus comes from six western-based, English language newspapers: *The New York Times* (NYT), *The Wall Street Journal* (WSJ), *The Washington Post* (WaPo), *The Financial Times* (FT), *The Guardian*, and *The Times*; and two Hong Kong-based, English language newspapers: the *China Daily* and the *South China Morning Post* (SCMP). Current NLP limitations of comparison across languages (Bender, 2009; Baden et al., 2021) made the challenge of including news sources in Cantonese and Mandarin formidable and resulted in the decision to include only English language newspapers (Earl et al., 2004).

NLP models often have inconsistent performance across languages (Lee, 2014; Du et al., 2018; Baden et al., 2021). While multilingual NLP approaches are being proposed, they are typically proven only for languages related to English (Mimno et al., 2009; Reber, 2019; Chan et al., 2020). In fact, Bender (2009) and Pires et al. (2019) discuss the limitations generally, and Baden et al. (2021) discuss specific issues in multilingual NLP for the social sciences. Moreover, a recent WMT shared task (Barrault et al., 2019) shows why translation as a preprocessing step is a suboptimal option (cf. Field et al., 2018) as current translation systems struggle to maintain coherence across long document contexts. These NLP limitations are the fundamental reasons why only English-language newspapers have been chosen as the sources of our article corpus, a few other factors further validate our choice. English is one of the two official languages of Hong Kong (Basic Law, Article 9), with 51.9% of the population speaking it. Then, the SCMP and China Daily are the printed English language newspapers with the largest readership in Hong Kong. Finally, our choice of relying on selected Hong Kong English language newspapers is consistent with the work of Bhatia (2015), Yu (2015); Wong and Liu (2018); Du et al. (2018) and Lee (2014), who also use English language news sources to investigate selected episodes of protests in Hong Kong.

We use news articles focusing on eight non-randomly selected episodes of civic unrest in Hong Kong to compare their news values and newsworthiness in the volatile political setting of post-handover Hong Kong. We focus on (i) the 1998–2002 July anniversary marches; (ii) the 2003 protests against the national security bill; (iii) the 2004–2019 July 1 protests; (iv) the 2006 Star and Queen protests; (v) the 2012 protests against a Moral and National Education; (vi) the 2014 Occupy Central protests; (vii) the 2016 Riots; and (viii) the 2019–2020 anti-ELAB protests. Taken together, these protests represent a sustained citizens' effort to safeguard Hong Kong from the loss of civil and political liberties (Sparks, 2015; Chan, 2015).

The articles were collected through keyword-based searches in ProQuest Newspapers for western English language newspapers, and Newsbank Access World News Research Collection for Hong Kong English language newspapers. We searched for the keywords "Hong Kong" + "protests", "Hong Kong" + "rallies", "Hong Kong" + "marches", and "Hong Kong" + "riots". We used the East Coast edition for the NYT and WSJ, the UK edition for the FT, The Guardian, and The Times, and Hong Kong edition for China Daily. We chose the printed rather than online editions of these newspapers because printed edition are everlasting and unchanging, whereas online editions update published articles thus making it difficult, if not impossible, for the reader and the research to refer to or retrieve the original version. To be eligible for collection, articles had to be at least 300 words long, and focus on the protests. A one-by-one, manual screening process eliminated irrelevant items such as eventual duplicates within each publication, readers' letters, and articles that included any of the chosen keywords but whose content was not about the protests. Following the manual screening, we retained 793 articles from western–based newspapers and 3729 from Hong Kong–based newspapers, with a mean length of 783 tokens. A total 4522 articles make up the *Hong Kong Protest News Dataset* (©DoreGMD), the original curated collection that informs our research.

The *Hong Kong Protest News Dataset* has a 22-year time horizon, spanning from January 1, 1998 to June 30, 2020, to capture changes in how selected Hong Kong- and western-based newspapers covered protests in Hong Kong, and to test the meaning and robustness of eventual changes of how newspapers treated protests over time. The extended time horizon together with the size of our sample departs from current research practice, which favors the treatment of smaller samples of

Table 2.1 Comparable Hong Kong protest news datasets

Author	Protest event	No. of articles	News source
Bhatia (2015)	Occupy Central	100	SCMP
Yu (2015)	Occupy Central	249	SCMP, NYT, The Times, The Guardian
Wong and Liu (2018)	Occupy Central	875	China Daily, SCMP
Du et al. (2018)	Occupy Central	191	FT, NYT, Ming Pao, People's Daily, United Daily News
Lee (2014)	HK Protests, 2001–2012	1,767	Apple Daily, The Oriental, Ming Pao

Source: Authors

articles, generally in the hundreds rather than the thousands, focuses on a particular episode of protest, or compares no more than two protests at different points in time.

Table 2.1 contrasts the scope and scale of our dataset with previous corpora focused on protests in Hong Kong. Bhatia (2015), for instance, uses approximately 100 articles the SCMP published over the last 2 months of the 2014 Occupy Central protests to understand the SCMP's characterization of those protests. Yu (2015) uses 249 news stories to examine the frames that the SCMP, the NYT, and The Guardian used in their coverage of the 2014 Occupy Central protests. Wong and Liu (2018) examine newspapers' representations of the aggressive behavior of social actors in the 2014 Occupy Central protests based on 875 articles from the China Daily and the SCMP. Du et al. (2018) rely on 191 articles from the FT, the NYT, Ming Pao, People's Daily, and the United Daily News to show how differently these newspapers framed news stories about the 2014 Occupy Central protests. Lee (2014) uses 1767 articles from the Apple Daily, the Oriental, and Ming Pao to investigate whether news organizations exercised any social control function in their discussion of protests that took place in Hong Kong between 2001 and 2012.

As newspaper coverage remains one of the most useful records of protest events (Earl et al., 2004), we took steps to include a diverse array of news sources, keeping in mind Hallin and Mancini's (2004) framework for comparing media systems worldwide, while also remaining aware that Chinese, North American and British newspapers sit at the opposite ends of the spectrum in terms of ownership and state control.

Despite the commercialization of the media in China, including Hong Kong-SAR, "national, provincial and local newspapers remain under the control of the Chinese Communist Party (CCP) and/or the government as in the case of Xinhua News Agency or the China Daily" (Shirk, 2011: 9). Article 27 of the Basic Law states that "Hong Kong residents shall have freedom of speech, of the press, and of publication,"[1] thus acknowledging the right to maintain freedom of the press and expression in Hong Kong. The existing legal framework, however, does not provide unequivocal protection for press freedom. The National People's Congress of China,

[1] https://www.basiclaw.gov.hk/en/basiclaw/index.html

in fact, holds the right to interpret the Basic Law,[2] and laws and provisions that can be used to suppress press freedom continue to exist, an unfortunate legacy of the British colonial years. In fact, British Hong Kong was not a free press haven as commonly believed. The colonial government had laws in place that gave sweeping power to control and punish news organizations when contents were deemed seditious and anti-government. Shen states that "there were as many as 30 laws in Hong Kong that could be used to curb media freedom" (1972: 31), including the *Seditious Publication Ordinance* (enacted 1914), the *Printers and Publications Ordinance* (first enacted 1886, amended 1927), the *Chinese Publications (Prevention) Ordinance* (1907), the *Emergency Regulations (Amendment) Ordinance* (1949), and the *Control of Publications (Consolidation) Ordinance* (1951). According to the 1997 Annual Report by the Hong Kong Journalists Association, these were the same laws British authorities had in place in other colonies to ensure that free speech, free assembly, and free association could not be used to challenge colonial authority or oppose British rule and interests.

While the British colonial administration seldom applied these laws, the few cases in which they did were against the leftist press. One of the most prominent cases was the March 1, 1952 incident, when Wen Wei Po, Ta Kung Pao, and the New Evening Post were prosecuted for "publishing libelous materials that stirred up hatred or contempt against the government" (Ngok, 2007: 952), after they published a People's Daily article criticizing the colonial government for failing to provide relief for the victims of a fire which destroyed a temporary refugee shelter. Another one involved the conviction of Afternoon News, Hong Kong Evening News, and Tin Fung Daily News, during the 1967 riots, for stirring anti-government sentiments and false reporting. Because laws were only rarely invoked, the British administration had "to rely on a combination of cajolery and manipulation to corral the press in order to prevent dissent at the margin from percolating into the mainstream" (Hutcheon, 1998: 6). British authorities employed co-optation and rewarded publishers of pro-government newspapers with British medals of honor and lucrative advertisement contracts. The colonial government also used the Government Information Service to *control* news flow through "selective dissemination of government information to shape public opinion, closed-door briefings for selected reporters, and release of daily news bulletins" (Lee & Chan, 1990: 125–139). These bulletins often became newspaper articles due to both lax professional standards and newspapers' desire to maintain a good relationship with the colonial government.

Under colonial administration, Hong Kong enjoyed a free press reputation mostly because it allowed—*though surveilled*—the publication of a full spectrum of ideological positions, ranging from papers sponsored by the Kuomintang (KMT) such as the Hong Kong Times, to those funded by the Chinese Communist Party (CCP), such as the Ta Kung Pao. Moreover, as the KMT-CCP split was the major political cleavage in Hong Kong before the 1980s, the colonial government welcomed newspapers' obsessive focus on this ideological struggle as it directed public

[2] http://english.www.gov.cn/archive/white_paper/2014/08/23/content_281474982986578.htm

attention to international rather domestic affairs. As before the 1980s, the relationship between the colonial administration and the press was one of controlled pluralism, the press was free to report on social and economic news, but not to criticize the colonial administration. The signing of the 1984 Joint Sino-British Declaration formalized the framework and timetable for Hong Kong's return to China, and in an effort to lessen Hongkongers' concerns over the issue of post-1997 freedoms, British authorities began *disappearing* the draconian press laws they had set in place. While progress was slow due to China's unwillingness to cooperate in window-dressing the colonial reputation for freedom of the press, in March 1987 colonial authorities repealed the *Control of Publications Consolidation Ordinance*, a law that conferred the authorities with wide-ranging powers over the media. In 1991, the British colonial authorities introduced a Bill of Rights, which for the first time expressly guaranteed freedom of expression, mostly to address fears that Hong Kong would witness democratic suppression similar to the one seen in China in 1989. However, in February 1997, Beijing announced that the bill would be adjusted after the handover to ensure it did not undermine pre-existing legislation nor restrict the scope for future law making.

By July 1, 1997, 30 offending sections from 17 acts that the British administration believed to contain the majority of the press control laws had been written off. However, the Hong Kong Journalists Association argued that "a legal platform still existed which could be used to limit the free press, and that the outgoing colonial government had failed to convert its administrative code on access to government information into a freedom of information law" (Hutcheon, 1998: 6–7).

The political transition kicked off by the Sino-British negotiations brought significant changes to the Hong Kong media environment. The politicization brought on by the negotiations meant that Hong Kong's political development, rather than the KMT–CCP rivalry, would become a press priority. Seeing the media as vital for propaganda, Beijing weaved its own web of co-optation by providing banquets and gifts, appointing media chiefs into Beijing's appointed institutions, and appealing to patriotism as shown in Table 2.2. After the transfer of sovereignty in 1997, Chinese authorities sought to reduce critical noise against Beijing in the Hong Kong printed media while *respecting* press freedom. Chinese authorities sought to influence the local media through business alliances, as some family-run newspapers were purchased by business tycoons around the 1997 handover.[3] The tycoons believed that a media investment could pay dividends, without having to risk their outlets'

[3] In the post-1997 era, the most prominent acquisition was probably that of the Hong Kong Economic Journal, a daily known for its independence, in-depth analysis, and bold criticism. In late 2006, PCCW chairman Richard Li Tzar-kai, the son of tycoon Li Ka-shing, spent HK$280 million to acquire 50% of the Journal from its founder Lam Shan-muk and his wife Lok Yau-mui. Media reports of the deal highlighted the public fear that Li's investment would put its editorial independence at risk, though Li more than once publicly denied that he would intrude into the editorship.

Table 2.2 Media-related Chinese appointments to Hong Kong's advisory bodies

	Position	Title
Louis Cha	Ming Pao Group Founder	Basic Law Consultative Committee, Basic Law Drafting Committee, HKSAR Preparatory Committee
Wan-fung Chan	Wen Wei Pao former deputy editor in chief	Basic Law Consultative Committee Hong Kong Member of the Chinese People's Political Consultative Conference, Selection Committee for the first government of HKSAR
Deacon Te-Ken Chiu	Asia Television director	Hong Kong Member of the Chinese People's Political Consultative Conference
Yei-ching Chow	Television Broadcasts Ltd. Director	Selection Committee for the first government of HKSAR
Yi-min Fu	Ta Kung Pao former publisher	Basic Law Drafting Committee, Hong Kong Deputy to the National People's Congress
Mona Fong	Television Broadcasts Ltd. Deputy chairperson	Selection Committee for the first government of HKSAR
Nick Griffin	Television Broadcasts Ltd. Former principal reporter	Basic Law Consultative Committee
Man-fat Ho	Sing Pao publisher	Basic Law Consultative Committee
Sai-chu Ho	Tin Tin Daily News Director	Hong Kong Member of the Chinese People's Political Consultative Conference, Selection Committee for the first government of HKSAR
Ting-kwan Ho	Television Broadcasts Ltd. director and general manager	Basic Law Consultative Committee
Chu-jen Hu	Pai Hsing semi-monthly editor in chief	Basic Law Consultative Committee
Hock-nien Kuok	South China Morning Post chairman	Hong Kong Affairs Advisor
Cho-jat Lee	Hong Kong Commercial Newspaper Co Ltd. Chairman	Hong Kong Member of the Chinese People's Political Consultative Conference, Preparatory Committee for HKSAR, Selection Committee for the first government of HKSAR
Tse-chung Lee	Wen Wai Pao former publisher	Hong Kong Member of the Chinese People's Political Consultative Conference
Lik Ma	Hong Kong Commercial Daily deputy publisher	Hong Kong Affairs Advisor
Chun-leung Poon	Sing Tao Man Pao former editor in chief	Basic Law Consultative Committee
Chiu-yin Pun	Commercial Radio former assistant general manager	Basic Law Consultative Committee
Tak-sing Tsang	Ta Kung Pao former editor in chief	NPC, Preparatory Committee for HKSAR Selection Committee for the first government of HKSAR
Guo-hua Wong	Ta Kung Pao publisher	Hong Kong Member of the Chinese People's Political Consultative Conference

Source: Official NPC and CPPCC data; Civil Miscellaneous Lists, Hong Kong Government

independence by explicitly tilting toward the Chinese authorities.[4] Moreover, given that newspaper ownership never amounted to a financial burden for these business tycoons, "they could afford a certain degree of reader attrition that the adjustment of their media content may create" (Lee, 2007: 32).

As a result, developments such as "infiltration of Chinese and pro-China capital into the media system" (Lee, 2018: 9), "shifts in journalistic paradigms" (Chan & Lee, 1989: 97), and media self-censorship (Fung & Lee, 1998) became more relevant and pronounced over time. Beginning in the early 1990s, these processes changed journalistic practices in Hong Kong, slowly altering the boundaries of the in-print media discourse between Hong Kong-based newspapers and the Chinese and Hong Kong governments, and steadily, although subtly, eroding press freedom. Nevertheless, in the interest of demonstrating the feasibility of the principles of *one country, two systems,*[5] Beijing largely held back from openly intervening in Hong Kong affairs in the first few years after 1997. This did not mean that the Chinese government did not try to control the Hong Kong press. Chinese government officials set up the limits of acceptable press coverage by "stating a three *no* policy for the Hong Kong media: no advocacy for Taiwan/Tibet independence, no engagement in subversive activities, and no personal attack on national leaders" (Lee & Chu, 1998: 70–71), and also by relying on various strategies to induce press self-censorship.[6]

Three of these strategies are particularly noteworthy. First, the Chinese government would try to influence the Hong Kong press through co-opting media owners, who may have business interests in mainland China (Lee & Chu, 1998). The owners may not dictate daily news operation, but they can exercise influence through making allocative decisions regarding the use of resources, or the hiring of top-level personnel. While it remains difficult to ascertain the extent to which these kinds of decisions could have been politically motivated, as long as journalists understood them as such, they signaled what may and/or may not be appropriate. As such, "these decisions effectively set up norms for news coverage" (Lee, 2007: 137).

Second, Beijing's comments on and criticisms towards the Hong Kong media set up "norms of political correctness" (Kwong, 2015: 278). In October 2000, for instance, in response to a question from a Hong Kong journalist about the Central government's attitude towards the Chief Executive election, then Chinese President Jiang Zemin criticized the journalist and the Hong Kong press as "too simple, sometimes naive".[7] Through overt criticisms from Chinese officials the Hong Kong press learnt what would irritate China, which, in turn, would push the boundaries of press freedom and journalistic professionalism (Lau & To, 2002).

---

[4] The Ming Pao and the party-owned Guangzhou Daily have jointly published the North America Special Edition of Guangzhou Daily.

[5] See footnote no. 6

[6] Media self-censorship refers to "a set of editorial actions committed by media organizations aiming to curry favor and avoid offending the power stakeholders such as the government, advertisers and major business corporations." (Lee & Chan, 2009: 112).

[7] http://edition.cnn.com/TRANSCRIPTS/0010/27/wv.02.html

Third, the Chinese government employed "strategic ambiguity" (Cheung, 2003: 210–225) to induce self-censorship by giving out warnings without defining key terms or identifying topics that should not be discussed. The Chinese government, for instance, repeatedly warned the Hong Kong media not to *advocate* for Taiwan's independence without clarifying the difference between *advocating* and *reporting* about Taiwan affairs. Strategic ambiguity widens the space between what is and is not allowed *journalistically* while at the same time increasing the space for self-censorship. Hong Kong journalists and newspapers have established *strategic rituals* (Lee, 2007) to limit and manage the impact of strategic ambiguity. These include juxtapositions between positive and negative views towards the power holders, the use of polls as objective indicators of public opinions, the adoption of rhetorical strategies to construct neutral and objective narratives, emphasis on hard facts, and the formal titles of people who act as news sources. While useful, strategic rituals could both help and hurt. They can constrain diversity of opinions and merely be self-censorship in disguise rather than a shield against undue political influence (Glasser, 1992; Tuchman & Tuchman, 1978).

After the 1997 handover, perceptions of self-censorship became widespread among journalists, together with the concern that what started out as self-conscious self-censorship may have become the norm over time. In fact, as Hong Kong journalists interact with Chinese officials more frequently and regularly, they may become more sympathetic towards the mainland and the Chinese government, with news media becoming more careful in rendering judgments of China and China-related issues. This can be understood as a process of *cultural co-orientation,*[8] which may result in journalists' views shifting gradually closer to China's official views and coverage of national issues becoming less problematic. The interplay of *co-optation*, *strategic interactions*, *cultural co-orientation*, and *self-censorship* proves how the press in Hong Kong can be plied, and its freedom limited, without the need for formal and overt control from Beijing.

In contrast with the realities of the Hong Kong media, the North American and British media landscapes have been characterized by the centrality of large-scale cultural industries since the development of the penny press in the 1830s.[9] For several decades in the mid-twentieth century, an equilibrium existed in the media system. Stable markets made the dominant media companies highly profitable and very influential as social institutions. Newspapers invested heavily in newsrooms, and the journalist profession grew in autonomy and influence. Journalism was characterized by a low level of "political parallelism" (van der Pas et al., 2017: 493) with the norm of objectivity dominating journalistic ethics, and most news organizations avoiding identification with political parties. Over time, economic, technological,

[8] Following a tradition in communication research focusing on balance, congruence and convergence, co-orientation is understood as "the acquisition of better information and achievement of increased understanding between two individuals or groups through interactions, which may lead to convergence in attitudes towards external objects and mutual agreement on issues" (McQuail & Windahl, 1993: 27–37).

[9] https://www.britannica.com/topic/publishing/Era-of-the-Industrial-Revolution

and political change began disrupting those very elements that had guaranteed the stability and fairness of the press system in the late twentieth century. Stable boundaries that once separated markets have been disrupted by digital convergence and deregulation. Changing business models have impacted newsrooms' sizes, and the Internet has accelerated the fragmentation of broadcast industries. Political parallelism has increased, and newspapers have become more inclined to adopt partisan identities, with little concern about the reporting pitfalls of adopting such clear-cut political orientation, including declining public trust.

Chapter 3
Non-rhetorical Tactics

A contextualized view of the volume and timing or news articles published between 1998 and 2020 strengthens the understanding of the news value and thematic relevance of the protests to Hong Kong– and western-based newspapers. The overview and discussion presented in this chapter anchors the findings and discussion that we present in Chap. 4.

3.1 Volume and Timing of Articles on Hong Kong Protests

Protests are an important means in contemporary societies for citizens to voice their opinions and concerns and exercise their right to free speech. Most protests, however, happen at specific times and places, and are witnessed by relatively small numbers of people. As such, protests' ability to communicate their messages and achieve their desired outcomes depends on whether and how the press portrays them (Agnone, 2007; King, 2011). While "there is no easy formula that can determine whether something is newsworthy" (Lorenz & Vivian, 1996: 22), there is agreement that features such as "unusual, timely, local or nearby, surprising, about change, conflict and people, has impact, evokes human interest, and conveys information" (Cotter, 2010: 68) make events valuable to the press. Protests are a natural fit to these parameters, and thus inherently newsworthy (Liebes & Blum-Kulka, 2004). After all, *if it bleeds, it leads* (Altheide, 2018).

Press coverage, however, can be a double-edged sword. It can either amplify and legitimize the protesters' voices, thus enhancing the chances for a protest to enlist public support and influence authorities (Gamson & Wolfsfeld, 1993), or marginalize and delegitimize protests by portraying them as dangerous or irrelevant (Boykoff, 2006). In this regard, the volume and timing of articles about protests in

G. M. D. Dore et al., *A Free Press, If You Can Keep It*, SpringerBriefs in Political Science,
https://doi.org/10.1007/978-3-031-27584-5_3

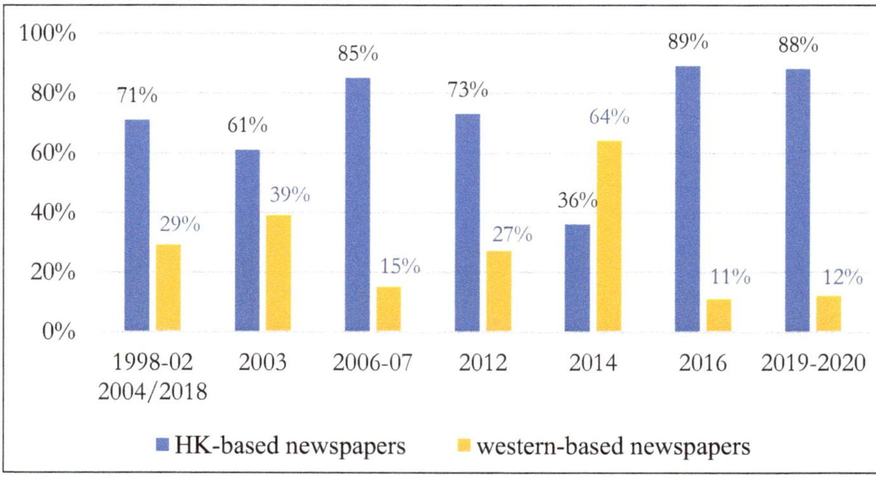

Fig. 3.1 1998–2020: Hong Kong– and western-based newspaper coverage of protests. (Source: Authors)

Hong Kong make it possible to gauge the news value of protests as well as the thematic relevance to newspapers in general.[1]

Figure 3.1 shows that Hong Kong protests have been and continue to be newsworthy for both Hong Kong- and western-based newspapers. With 3347 articles, the SCMP published almost 8.8 times more articles than the China Daily (i.e., 3347 vs. 381), and more than any other newspapers in the *Hong Kong Protest News Dataset.* Moreover, the SCMP and China Daily together published 4.7 times more articles than the NYT, WSJ, WaPo, FT, the Guardian, and the Times combined (i.e., 3728 vs. 793). Except for 2014, between 1998 and 2020, the SCMP and the China Daily published more, and more consistently, about protests in Hong Kong than any other newspaper. Western-based newspapers' coverage, instead, declines over time, is punctuated by sharp peaks and dips, and is dominated by the NYT, which with 425 articles, published more than half of what all western-based newspapers published about Hong Kong protests.

As the main English-language printed newspapers in Hong Kong, it is not surprising that the SCMP and China Daily cover Hong Kong matters is more frequently and voluminously than western-based newspapers. This is particularly so nowadays as the foreign press has reduced the space, resources and commitment devoted to the topics it covers and cut back on-the-ground reporting of foreign news. But even then, it is a lot of difference. Moreover, the ample and sustained coverage of the

[1] Research on news values implies answering a fundamental question: "What is news?" and journalism and communication-related disciplines have put significant effort in trying to answer this question. See Galtung & Ruge, 1965; Eilders, 2006; Welbers et al., 2016.

protests enabled the SCMP and the China Daily to curb plurality of views and set the agenda on the salience of the protests.

For instance, 2016 was a year punctuated by multiple protests, including those against a new election procedure requiring candidates running for the LegCo elections to sign a form "acknowledging Hong Kong as an inseparable part of China."[2] Between February and September 2016, the SCMP and the China Daily published a total of 318 articles (280 and 38), whereas the six western-based newspapers together published 37 articles over the same timeline. In the case of the 2019–2020 anti-ELAB protests, between late March and May, the SCMP published 166 articles, whereas over the same period of time, western-based newspapers published three articles: two in the NYT and one in WSJ. These coverage trends allowed the SCMP and the China Daily to focus almost entirely on the confrontational and violent aspects of the protests. The 59 articles that the SCMP published between mid-March and the end of April focus on the negative consequences of civil unrest. The 95 articles the SCMP published in May 2019 relentlessly focused on anti-ELAB scuffles, heated confrontations, and citizens' vocal opposition to ELAB. These trends continued over June 4–14, 2019, when the SCMP published 234 articles and the China Daily 14. In contrast, western-based newspapers covered the anti-ELAB unrest inconsistently; altogether they only published 80 articles between March and June 2019, with the NYT publishing more than any other western-based newspapers included in our dataset. By the time western-based media began paying systematic attention to what was happening in Hong Kong, the SCMP and the China Daily had set the agenda on the coverage of the anti-ELAB protests. Their agenda fitted the canons of the protest paradigm to the detriment of the international media's efforts to legitimize the democratic demands of the citizens of Hong Kong.

Finally, 2014 emerges as an exception in how much coverage western- and Hong Kong-based newspapers dedicated to the protests that were held in the Hong Kong Central district for 79 days,[3] with western-based newspapers publishing 55% more articles than Hong Kong- based ones (i.e., 236 vs. 131). The scale, involvement of conflict and compelling visuals of the Occupy Central protests captured western media interest with an intensity seldom seen before, with their news value enhanced by how reminiscent they were of the large-scale, pro-democracy protests which swept the Middle East and other countries around the world between 2010 and 2011.[4] The SCMP and China Daily's scant coverage of the Occupy Central protests can, instead, be seen as *self-censorship* in response to Beijing's strategic ambiguity over what should and should not be covered. As the Occupy Central protests continued for 79 days, they became China's most challenging political struggle since the Beijing June 4, 1989 protests.[5] It is perhaps not surprising, then, that Hong Kong

[2] https://carnegie-mec.org/2016/10/17/implications-of-sixth-hong-kong-legislative-election-for-relations-with-beijing-pub-64872

[3] See page 6.

[4] https://www.britannica.com/event/Arab-Spring

[5] https://www.britannica.com/event/Tiananmen-Square-incident

journalists began to exercise more than a modicum of caution in how they covered the protests.

3.2 Does News Coverage *Granger-Cause* Protest Size?

Snow and Benford (1988) and Gans (2004) discuss whether news organizations can be considered responsible for the effects of the contents they publish. Chan and Lee propose a "conceptual distinction between the media serving as 'facilitators' (…) and as 'mobilizing agents' in collective action" (2008: 217). Their work questions the correctness of stating that newspapers *mobilize* citizens. They argue that "being a facilitator does not require the media organization to have any particular attitude towards a protest beyond the judgment of its newsworthiness (…) whereas a media organization can be regarded as a mobilizing agent when it exhibits a supportive attitude towards a protest, which may influence the readers' participatory decision" (2008: 218). Their scholarly work concludes that investigating whether the media play a facilitator or mobilizer role could be revealing of citizens' access to free speech as well as freedom of the press.

Building on Freeman's (1983) work on times series analysis of political relationships and Lee's (2006) research on the collective efficacy of protests, we hypothesize the existence of correlations between news coverage and protests' size, which in turn would help us understand whether the SCMP and the China Daily served as *facilitators* and/or *mobilizing agents* vis-à-vis protests. To investigate this hypothesis, we employ Granger causality (1980)—an econometric test used to verify the usefulness of one variable to in forecasting another. We should note that while *causality* is in the name, *Granger causality* posits no causal model but rather measures levels of correlation between time series in terms of predictive utility. In its basic definition, Granger causality supposes at least three terms, Xt, Yt, and Wt, and attempts to forecast Xt + 1 using past terms of Xt and Wt. Then, it tries to forecast Xt + 1 using past terms of Xt, Yt, and Wt. If the second forecast is found to be more successful, then the past of Y appears to contain information helpful in forecasting Xt + 1 that is not in past Xt or Wt. We designed two case studies based on the SCMP, China Daily, and western-based newspapers' coverage of the 2019 anti-ELAB protests. The first case study focuses on the protests that took place between February and May 2019, following the announcement of the proposed amendment to the extradition bill. The second case study looks at the protests that took place between June 4 and 14, 2019, in reaction to both Chief Executive Lam's determination to keep the ELAB on the legislative agenda and her statements comparing the protests to the actions of capricious children.[6] The protests that unfolded over the weeks between mid-February and the end of May 2019, and those of June 4–14, 2019 lend

[6] https://www.scmp.com/news/hong-kong/politics/article/3014250/hong-kong-chief-executive-carrie-lam-accuses-anti

themselves well to investigate the existence of correlations between news coverage and protests' size because of the protests' extended timeline and the newspapers' voluminous coverage of them.

Following Field et al. (2018), we computed daily article-level metrics, namely the number of articles published each day across the timeline, from February to June 14, 2019 and identified estimates for citizens' participation in the protests that took place over that period of time. To account for differences in the available estimates of protests' size, we used estimates taken at the peak of each protest event, a data point for which there is consistency across news sources. Then, we calculated the percentage change of these series, controlled for long term effects, and focused on short-term effects. We run the Granger causality analysis by fitting a linear regression model to the time series data.[7] Fig. 3.2 shows that for both case studies

2A. Protest Events and Newspaper Coverage between February and May 2019

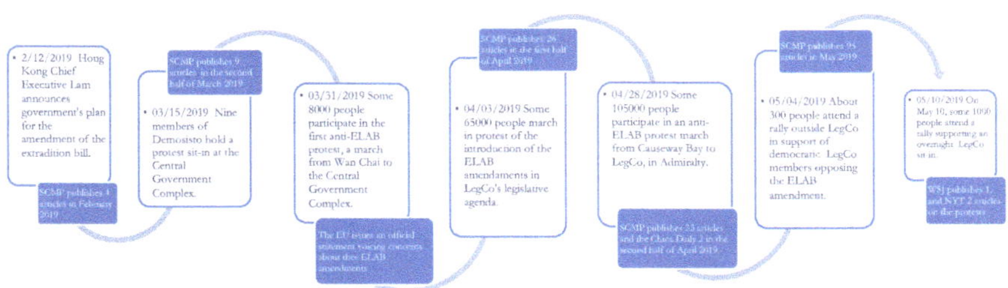

Table 2.A. Newspaper Coverage and Protest Sizes between February and May 2019

	1 Lag	p-value (≤ 0.05)	2 Lag	p-value (≤ 0.05)
wt−1	0.227	0.003	0.024	0.007
rt−1	0.325	0.005	0.319	0.001

2B. Protest Events and Newspaper Coverage between June 4 and 14, 2019

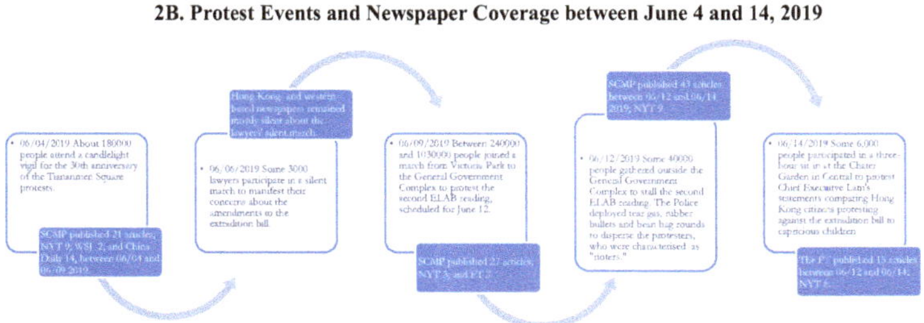

Table 2.B. Newspaper Coverage and Protest Sizes between June 4 and 14, 2019

	1 Lag	p-value (≤ 0.05)	2 Lag	p-value (≤ 0.05)
wt−1	0.422	0.002	0.064	0.002
rt−1	0.221	0.001	0.219	0.005

Fig. 3.2 Granger causality analysis of the 2019 anti-ELAB protests. (Source: Authors)

[7] $$C(w_t) = \sum_{m}^{i=1} \alpha_i \left(C(w_{t-1}) \right) + \sum_{n}^{j=1} \beta_j \left(C(r_{t-j}) \right)$$

an increase in news coverage is followed by an increase in citizens' participation in the protests. We paired these findings with a content review of the articles published in the SCMP, China Daily, and western-based newspapers between February and June 2019, to establish whether the SCMP, the China Daily or western-based newspapers played a *facilitator* or a *mobilizer* role vis-à-vis the anti-ELAB protests.

Our review found that, between late March and May 2019, the SCMP and the China Daily published 166 articles, and that between June 4 and 14 2019, these two news outlets published three times as many articles as western-based newspapers (i.e., 248 to 80). While the SCMP and the NYT published more than any other newspapers in our dataset, the SCMP published five times as many articles as the NYT (i.e., 234 vs. 45). Qualitative content analysis shows that throughout their coverage, both the SCMP, the China Daily and western-based newspapers consistently focus on the violence and disruptiveness of the protests. However, the SCMP and the China Daily did so to leverage the news value of the negative consequences, particularly economic and financial ones, of civil unrest for Hong Kong. Instead, western-based newspapers highlighted the protests' radical tactics and pervasive violence as "the most effective means for protesters to be heard" (Ma, 2007: 201), which in turn points to a "supportive attitude towards a protest, which may influence the readers participatory decision" (McCluskey et al., 2009: 306). These editorial choices suggest that the western-based newspapers played both a *facilitating* and *mobilizing* role vis-à-vis the protests which took place between February and June 2019, whereas the SCMP and the China Daily played solely a *facilitating* role vis-à-vis the anti-ELAB protests. This finding confirms empirically that "the state-press relationship after the handover was under the dynamics of 'constant negotiation amidst self-restraint'" (Ma, 2007: 949) to manage Beijing's strategic ambiguity and co-option efforts.

Chapter 4
Rhetorical Tactics

News article content analysis helps identify and understand shifts in journalistic practices. As such it can be indicative of the degree of press freedom that countries experience. In this chapter, we investigate this in terms of framing choices, lexical choice, and the manner of lexical use, and we contextualize our discussion with the findings showcased in Chap. 3.

4.1 The Protest Paradigm: Framing the Protests

The SCMP and the China Daily covered protests using the *protest paradigm* (Weaver & Scacco, 2013; Boyle et al., 2012). This is a pattern of coverage that, while varying in degree, focuses on the deviant, threatening, and violent aspects of protests that challenge the status quo, and invokes public opinion against the protests. When applying the protest paradigm, "newspapers tend to borrow the script of crime news, highlights the protesters' (strange) appearance and/or ignorance, portrays protests as ineffective, focuses on the theatrical aspects of the protests" (McLeod & Hertog, 1998: 190–194). In this chapter, we give computational credence to the manner in which the SCMP and the China Daily employ the protest paradigm in their coverage of Hong Kong protests between 1998 and 2020.

One of the most powerful elements of the protest paradigm is the way in which protest news stories are *framed*. Entman explains that "framing essentially involves selection and salience. To frame is to select some aspects of a perceived reality and make them more salient in a communicating text, in such a way as to promote a particular problem definition, causal interpretation, moral evaluation, and/or treatment recommendation for the item described" (1993: 52). Identifying which frames the printed press uses to talk about protests in Hong Kong is a formidable challenge, due to the dynamic political and social context in which protests may happen and evolve over time. As what is included is as important as what is excluded, the frames

G. M. D. Dore et al., *A Free Press, If You Can Keep It*, SpringerBriefs in Political Science,
https://doi.org/10.1007/978-3-031-27584-5_4

chosen to organize news stories can have a powerful influence on public attitudes toward the protests. News construction, in fact, affects the meaning of news stories as certain topics and aspects of the news are emphasized over others (Entman, 2006; McCluskey et al., 2009; Chong & Druckman, 2007). Following past work (Boydstun et al., 2013; Jacobi et al., 2016; Dehler-Holland et al., 2021; Ylä-Anttila et al., 2022), we use topic models to find the frames used in the articles, then validate these. In its ability to characterize articles by the topics they contain, automatically identifying the topics from corpora, topic modeling helps understand the relative relevance that a wide variety of factors may play in framing the news that focused on Hong Kong protests between 1998 and 2020 (Gans, 2004; Shoemaker & Reese, 1996). As such, what emerges from the topic modeling analysis should be understood as frames—used as intended by Resnik[1]—unique and specific to coverage of the SCMP and China Daily of the protests in Hong Kong between 1998 and 2020.

We use latent Dirichlet allocation (LDA; Blei et al., 2003) for our topic models, which is a probabilistic generative model that maintains distributions over the words within each topic and the topics with each article, representing each article in the traditional vector space model (Salton et al., 1975). With LDA, we capture and convey the prevalence of various topics, so that we can contrast these across news sources and over time. We perform topic modeling with MALLET (McCallum, 2002), and to pre-process the articles, we lemmatize all tokens with WordNet's morphy feature (Miller, 1995), and also extract common bigrams. The resulting unigrams and bigrams were then converted to term–document matrices and provided as inputs to MALLET. We created models exploring varying numbers of automatically discovered topics in ranges we set for each subset of articles and re-evaluated the *coherence score* of resulting topics according to Mimno et al. (2011). In each case, we selected the model whose number of topics produced the highest coherence score and identified each of these topics with an identifying label. Our topic model represents each article as a mixture of topics. More prevalent topics have higher mixture weight, and the weights sum to 1 for each article—in LDA, these can be interpreted as samples from a k-dimensional Dirichlet distribution. We estimate a topic's prevalence in a news source or year by averaging the topic's weight across the articles from that source or year.

For the whole timeline of 1998–2020, we set the number of topics from $k = 5$ to 20. We found that using six topics produced the highest coherence score. The topics and their identifying labels are shown in Fig. 4.1. We treated the period 2019–2020 similarly, with the number of topics from $k = 7$ to 60. Figure 4.2 shows that, in this case, a 10-topic solution produced the highest coherence score. These topics and their identifying labels are in Fig. 4.2. Finally, for 2014, we set the number of topics from $k = 5$ to 20. For this subset of the articles, using five topics produced the highest coherence score. We then identified each topic with a label that interprets its lexical distribution. The labels were derived from inspecting both the most prevalent

[1]TADA 2021, 11th Annual Conference in New Directions in Analyzing Text as Data. Panel on *Longitudinal Studies of Language*, with Philip Resnik as discussant. https://tada2021.org

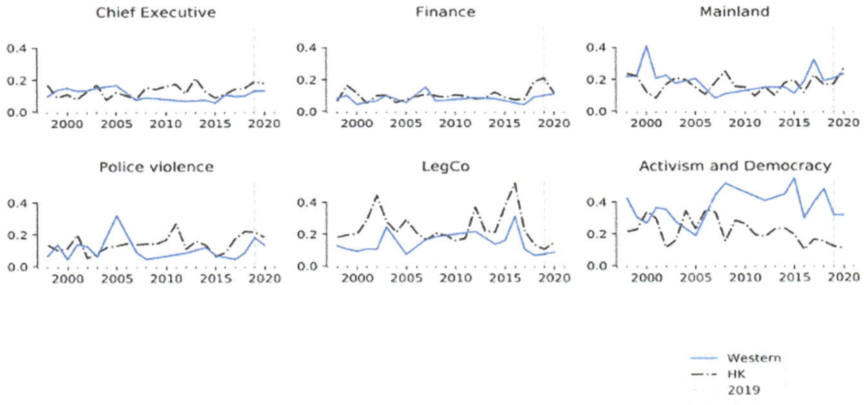

Topic	Top 10 words
Chief Executive	Bill, lam, extradition, public, court, executive, legal, case, cheng
Finance	Cent, per_cent, hk, business, company, market, million, property, trade, billion
Mainland	Beijing, Chinese, country, system, state, mainland, national, law, foreign, central
Public violence	Officer, station, violence, force, arrested, yesterday, students, road, university, day
LegCo	Election, party, leung, council, candidate, lawmaker, vote, executive, camp, legislative
Activism and democracy	Student, n't, movement, street, Chinese, leader, mr, day, Beijing, democracy

Fig. 4.1 Principal frames used in protest news construction in the SCMP, the China Daily and western-based newspapers between 1998 and 2020. (Source: Authors)

words in each topic, with the robustness of the findings being corroborated by spot check. We present these topics and their identifying labels in Fig. 4.3.

As shown in Fig. 4.1, our unsupervised topic modeling reveals that between 1998 and 2020, the SCMP and the China Daily used only six frames in their articles about protests in Hong Kong: *Chief Executive*, *Finance, Mainland*, *Police violence*, *LegCo*, and *Activism and Democracy*. In addition to the high coherence score, these topics have high predictive validity that is "measuring how well variation in topic usage correspondents with expected events" (Grimmer & Stewart, 2013: 21).

This finding is important in several respects. First, it is counterintuitive considering how protests in Hong Kong have changed over time. While protests have long been an undercurrent in Hong Kong's political culture, large-scale protests became more frequent, provocative, aggressive, and confrontational after 1997. Second, it is rhetorically skillful. The recurrency of a limited set of frames, known as *thematic framing*, increases the effectiveness of the protest paradigm in voicing criticism towards the protests in the abstract, without necessarily delegitimizing the act of protesting itself, nor directly criticizing Hongkongers as protesters (Aarøe & Petersen, 2018; Gross, 2008; Strange & Leung, 1999). For instance, the *Finance* frame focuses on the negative consequences that the protests have on Hong Kong as

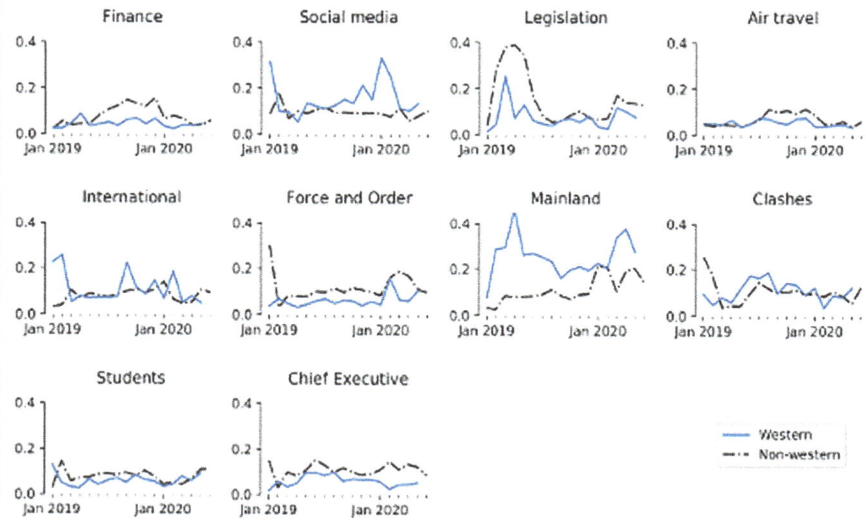

Topic	Top 10 words
Finance	Cent, per_cent, hk, market, property, billion, million, price, sale financial
Social media	N't, movement, young, have_been, political, do_n't, life, ha_been, hongkongers, social
Legislation	Extradition, Taiwan, lawmaker, council, election, chan,law, party, mainalnad, camp
Air travel	Business, mainland, airport, service, staff, august, day, company, tourist, cathay
International	China, Chinese, state, world, trade, united, Beijing, international, trump, mainland
Force and order	Officer, force, public, court, yesterday, case, arrested, law, post, source
Mainland	Beijing, law, China, system, national, country, Chinese, central, affair, two_system
Clashes	Station, officer, gas, tera, violence, road, Sunday, march, rally, tear_gas
Students	Student, university, school, group, campus, ho, education, support, event, more_than
Chief Executive	Lam, chief, executive, public, Carrie, Cheng, Carrie_Lam, extradition, political

Fig. 4.2 Principal frames used in protest news construction in the SCMP, the China Daily and western-based newspapers in 2019–2020. (Source: Authors)

an international financial hub and China's financial gateway and firewall. The *Mainland* frame highlights how the protests undermine Beijing's efforts to uphold the principles of *one country, two systems*.[2] The *Chief Executive* frame emphasizes how the protests undermine the government's duty to ensure that the rule of law prevails in Hong Kong, whereas the *Police Violence* frame stresses the police's duty to maintain order. From an editorial perspective, thematic framing makes it easier

[2] See footnote no. 6.

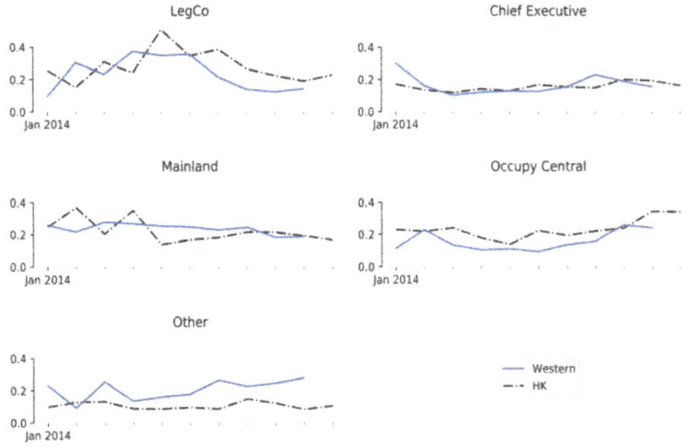

Topic	Top 10 words
LegCo	rule, candidate, occupy central, suffrage, country, reform, national, democratic, basic, vote
Chief Executive	Authority, talk, official, demonstration, force, make, washington, chung-ying, side, leung chung-ying
Mainland	year, mainland, party, communist, business, British, territory, London, UK, financial
Occupy Central	Site, he-said, road, admiralty, chan, mong, occupation, kok, mong kok
Other	Mr, publisher, city, york, Monday, demonstrator, Sunday, main, gas, tear

Fig. 4.3 Principal frames used in protest news construction in the SCMP, the China Daily and western-based newspapers in 2014. (Source: Authors)

for people to identify the issue at the heart of the protests as a society-wide phenomenon rather than citizens' discontent directed at specific actions of the Hong Kong administration.

Moreover, thematic framing also helps to better leverage the effectiveness of the protest paradigm. Qualitative content analysis conducted on a random sample of 25% of the articles from our corpus shows that in the case of the Mainland frame, the protest paradigm is used to highlight how the protests undermine Beijing's efforts to uphold the principles of one country, two systems: "the protest movement is trying to destroy one country two systems"[3]; "the protests challenged national sovereignty, threatened 'one country, two systems', and would destroy the city's prosperity and stability"[4]; within the Chief Executive frame, the protest paradigm is employed to emphasize how the protests undermine the Chief Executive and her government's duty to ensure that the rule of law prevails in Hong Kong: "this series of extremely violent acts is pushing Hong Kong to a very dangerous situation"[5];

[3] The South China Morning Post, July 28, 2019.

[4] The China Daily, August 16, 2019.

[5] The South China Morning Post, June 7, 2019.

"the protests are about resisting Chinese rule, delegitimatizing and destabilizing the Hong Kong rule of law",[6] whereas within the Police Violence frame to stress the police's duty to maintain order in the face of the growing frequency and violence of the protests: "months of street violence is already undermining both local and foreign-run businesses. The economy is taking a hit. Hong Kong has always been about being safe and rich"[7]; "The impact of these events, which began with peaceful mass protests, has been dramatic. Hong Kong's long-held reputation for the maintenance of law and order has been shattered. Its status as one of the world's safest cities has, at least temporarily, been lost."[8]

Topic modeling results for the 2019–2020 anti-ELAB protests reveal the SCMP and China Daily's continued use of thematic framing and consistency with the six frames used between 1998 and 2020. Within this consistency, we also see the emergence of a few frames unique to the anti-ELAB protests such as *Social Media*, *International*, and *Air Travel*, as shown in Fig. 4.2. *Social Media* became one of the hallmarks of the 2019–2020 anti-ELAB protests as they allowed and nurtured collective, horizontal decision-making. However, the SCMP and the China Daily used this frame to lament the negative implications of such use of social media. Both newspapers highlighted the need to regulate social media platforms in response to tow factors. The use of social media as shortcut to broaden the space for civic activism, and Beijing's helplessness toward such a difficult-to-counter accomplishment. The *International* frame emphasized Beijing's tendency to blame foreign forces, and especially the West, for domestic challenges—as in the case of the 1989 Tiananmen Square protests.[9] The use of this frame peaked four times, coinciding with some of the most violent episodes of the 2019–2020 protests and Beijing's and Hong Kong's officials openly accusing foreign countries of meddling in China's domestic affairs. This manifested as the SCMP and the China Daily pushing a narrative of the West harboring ulterior motives in its support of the protests.[10] Finally,

[6] The South China Morning Post, July 2, 2019.

[7] The China Daily, September 23, 2019.

[8] The South China Morning Post, November 28, 2019.

[9] These include statements of support for the protests from congressional leaders and Democratic presidential candidates and meetings between Hong Kong opposition figures and administration officials. Two such meetings that have been seized upon by China are one with a diplomat in the United States Consulate in Hong Kong, and another with Vice President Mike Pence and President Trump's national security adviser, John Bolton; see among others https://www.nytimes.com/2019/09/05/world/asia/china-hong-kong-protests.html

[10] "The belief that foreign forces, and especially the United States, were behind the Hong Kong protests feeds into a narrative that dates back to the Cold War, when the United States and the Soviet Union each sought to subvert the other's ideology and its proxy states with spies and subterfuge. Ideological rivalry has now subsided, with even China, though nominally still wedded to communism, showing no interest in exporting Marxism through subversion. But both Moscow and Beijing have in recent years sought to blame outsiders for domestic troubles—notably when Russia alleged that Michael McFaul, the American ambassador to Moscow from 2012 to 2014, was an instigator of street protests against Vladimir V. Putin, who was then the prime minister. China has until now mostly avoided attacking American diplomats by name, leaving this to nationalist bloggers like those who accused Jon M. Huntsman Jr., the former ambassador to Beijing, of trying

the use of the *Air Travel* frame highlighted the impact of the protests on Hong Kong International Airport and Hong Kong as a tourist destination. When using this frame, the SCMP and the China Daily insistently focused on the five-day protesters' sit-in that, between August 9 and 13, crippled air travel, brought the Hong Kong airport—which has been awarded world's best airport over 75 times since 1998—to a complete halt, and ended in violent physical confrontations, tear gas, and arrests (Ibrahim & Lam, 2020: 85).

While 2014 emerges as an exception in the volume of coverage that the SCMP and the China Daily dedicated to the Occupy Central protests, it does not represent an exception in terms of news framing. The results of the topic modeling for 2014, in fact, show that the SCMP and the China Daily employed thematic framing. Three of the five frames they used were consistent with the ones that the SCMP and the China Daily used to portray protests that took place between 1998 and 2020, and 2019–2020. As in the case of the 2019–2020 protests, our analysis reveals the emergence of a few frames, such as *Occupy Central* and *Other*, uniquely contextual to Occupy Central protests, which for 79 days captured news interest with a scale and intensity seldom seen before.

Figures 4.1, 4.2 and 4.3 also show that western-based newspapers used thematic framing, relying on the same six frames *–Chief Executive*, *Finance, Mainland, Police violence*, *LegCo*, and *Activism and Democracy*, to leverage the effectiveness of the protest paradigm in their characterization of protests. Yet, it is important to note that western-based newspapers used the protest paradigm in support of, rather than to the detriment of, the protests. In fact, in their characterization of the protests "as a pro-democracy revolution, as a fight for freedom and pluralism, the use of radical tactics and violence was seen as the most effective means for protesters to be heard." (McCluskey et al., 2009: 361). The treatment of the frame *Force and Order* in the context of the 2019 anti-ELAB protests helps illustrate these differences as well as the predictive validity of this frame. Figure 4.2 shows that in 2019–2020, the trends for the use of the *Force and Order* frame in Hong Kong– and western-based newspapers mimic each other, which points to the significance of this frame in the portrayal of the protests for both news sources. Between January 2019 and June 2020, coverage remains consistent across both news sources, even if the extent and peaks of coverage are significantly higher in Hong Kong– than in western-based newspapers. This is not surprising. According to the Minister for Security,[11] there were more than 1200 public order events (e.g., marches, demonstrations, or protests) from June to December 2019. While the protests were initially peaceful, over time they deteriorated into violent clashes between protesters and the Police, creating a cycle of violence that the Hong Kong government was not able to break. The Police used traditional riot control tactics, and on several occasions failed to

to stoke a "Jasmine Revolution" in China in 2011 by appearing outside a McDonald's restaurant in Beijing on the day of a proposed protest that never took place." The New York Times, August 8, 2019: https://www.nytimes.com/2019/08/08/world/asia/hong-kong-black-hand.html

[11] https://www.info.gov.hk/gia/general/202001/08/P2020010800638p.htm

distinguish between the majority of protesters who were peaceful, and the minority who turned to violence.

Public records show that the police fired 16,000 canisters of tear gas, 10,000 rubber bullets, 2000 bean bag rounds, and "arrested 7,700 protesters, 40% of whom were students" (Ng, 2020: 483). Perhaps predictably, the use of "indiscriminate" (Purbrick, 2019: 470) force by the Police against both violent and peaceful protesters to restore order emerges as a prominent news frame. Western-based newspapers, however, used the *Force and Order* frame to highlight the unprecedented level of the violence that characterized the police response to the protests, and how the police's violence could be a telling tale of Beijing's meddling to come in Hong Kong's affairs. Hong Kong-based newspapers used the *Force and Order* frame to offer detailed, chronicled descriptions of both the police's and protesters' actions, render the forceful responses as "an appropriate level of force to restore order and bring offenders to justice" (Ibrahim & Lam, 2020: 291), give space to the police statements and comments describing the Hong Kong violence as *home grown terrorism*, and promote a narrative aiming to restore a positive and trusting image of "Asia's finest" (Sinclair & Ng, 1997; Ibrahim & Lam, 2020: 289).

The findings of our research are unique to Hong Kong and are also consistent with earlier findings on the effects of repeated exposure to the same news frames, particularly when attempting to get ahead of other news outlets or setting an agenda. The use and relevance of repetitive news framing increases when the news stakes are high and value-laden, or contentious issues are reported—as is the case for protests in volatile political environments (Schulz et al., 2014). Repetitive thematic framing consistently changes the weight that is attached to certain news considerations over others, and is often followed by repetitive information-search which makes news pluralism less appealing and persuasive (Price et al., 1997; Shen, 2004; Valkenburg et al., 1999). By employing thematic framing, the SCMP and the China Daily make readers more likely to remember the arguments presented within a specific news frame, which increases the likelihood of readers agreeing with a frame's advocated standpoint (Fernandes, 2013; Baden & Lecheler, 2012; Stephens & Rains, 2011). Moreover, the repetitiveness, spaced over longer and longer periods of time, diminishes plurality of views about any particular protest, which combined with Hong Kong's slowly shifting journalistic paradigms results in an ever evolving challenge to press freedom in Hong Kong.

We tested the generalizability of our findings regarding the recurrent frames used in the SCMP and the China Daily against the Policy Frames Codebook of Boydstun et al. (2013). The Codebook, a reference to aid coding in computational content analysis "provides a general system for categorizing frames across policy issues (…) and contains 14 categories of frame 'dimensions' (plus an 'other' category) that are intended to be applicable to any policy issue and in any communication context" (2013: 4). As shown in Table 4.1, we found consistency over time, across eight of the fourteen categories listed in the Policy Frames Codebook.

Finally, as a complement to topic modeling identifying the most relevant news frames, we also used Linguistic Inquiry and Word Count (LIWC; Pennebaker et al.,

Table 4.1 Boydstun et al.'s policy frames and recurrent frames in news coverage of Hong Kong protests

Boydstun et al.'s policy frames	HK-and western-based newspapers frames		
	1998–2020	2019–2020	2014
Economic frames	Finance	Finance Air travel	–
Capacity and resources frames	–	–	–
Morality frames	Students	Activism and democracy	
Fairness and equality frames	–	–	–
Constitutionality and jurisprudence frames	LegCo	Legislation	LegCo
Policy prescription and evaluation	LegCo	Legislation	LegCo
Law and order, crime and justice frames	Police violence	Law and Order Clashes	–
Security and defense frames	–	–	–
Health and safety frames	–	–	–
Quality of life frames	–	–	–
Cultural identity frames	–	–	–
Public opinion frames	–	Social media	–
Political frames	Chief Executive	Chief Executive	Chief Executive
External regulation and reputation frames	Mainland	Mainland International	Mainland
Other frames	–	–	–

Source: Authors—adapted from the Policy Frames Codebook in Boydstun et al. (2013)

2015; Tausczik & Pennebaker, 2010) to analyze the language used in the articles. LIWC characterizes text based on word counts across more than 70 morphosyntactic and psychometric dimensions.

There were only discernible trends in two of these categories: "ASSENT" and "AFFILIATION." *Newspaper-ese* has some common stylistic elements across the world, and the subject matter we consider shares one focus: the protests in Hong Kong, which is likely to be the reason for the consistency both across LIWC categories and with our related findings. The "I" and "SHEHE" categories occur with similar frequency because of newspapers' aggregate tendencies to use first- or third-person pronouns with particular frequency. Meanwhile, the "INGEST" category, for instance, remains rare due to its irrelevance to the protests. Further, the LIWC categories include finite, pre-defined lists of words. We found that the word *fallout*, for instance, is not listed in the "NEGEMO" category, despite its negative connotation. Nevertheless, LIWC has value for validating later results that the SCMP and the China Daily use more negative words. In Table 4.2 we have bolded the negative emotion words most related to *tensions* in Hong Kong and western news sources. Even those present in LIWC highlight the contrast.

Table 4.2 Linguistic inquiry and word count (LIWC) analysis

Hong Kong-based newspapers	Western-based newspapers
Tensions	
Us-China, **tension**, **war**, dispute, **uncertainty**, heightened, prolonged, **worsening**, fallout, **turmoil**	Culture, state-owned, protections, tourists, market, base, rise, travel, closer, **argued**

10 nearest neighbors of *tensions*; words indicating negative emotion in LIWC (Pennebaker et al., 2015) are bolded. The western sources' use of *tensions* is more descriptive and impassive.

Source: Authors

4.2 BERT-MALLET *Vicinato* Plots

We have found the use of thematic framing across all newspapers in our sample as a means to reinforce the use of the protest paradigm, as manifested by the recurrency of frames identified through LDA. In this section, we aim to reinforce, validate, and give nuance to these findings. We introduce a novel methodology for visualizing topics derived from multiple levels of passage analysis, as well as articles covariates.

Topic models based on LDA depend on word frequencies but ignore higher-level syntactic structure—such as negation or idiom—and subword morphology. The fullest picture of news coverage patterns requires all three of these levels, though. In this section, we describe a novel visual method for incorporating all three. We connected lexically driven topic models (e.g., those created with MALLET) to deep, semantically driven topic models (e.g., those drawn from large language models paired with robust clustering methods) to explore the variation in our corpus. Each model recognizes separate aspects of the text, and the combination of weak signals from vintage and vogue models give a more complete perspective than any individual model. We use this in a way that explores the data, combining signals from two unsupervised models.

Traditional topic models fit distributions over term–document matrices, akin to factor analysis. But aspects of the text like misspelling, sentential context, and polysemy are ignored. A contrasting approach builds on pre-trained contextual language models (McCann et al., 2017; Peters et al., 2018). These models provide vectorial representations of text that are both distributed—in that salient information is spread across several dimensions of the vector instead of a symbolic structure and distributional—in that the vectors model how text appears in context. An advantage is that it does not require preprocessing the text (e.g., stemming, stop-word removal), as the context of each word is crucial to the model. A pre-trained contextual language model is a model whose parameters are already fitted to a large corpus, to optimize an objective function such as masked language modeling or next-sentence prediction (Devlin et al., 2019). Nevertheless, even without fine-tuning, these parameters are extremely useful as initializations for modeling other tasks like parsing, semantic role labelling, and part-of-speech tagging (Tenney et al., 2019) and modeling performance in high-stakes language assessment (McCarthy et al., 2021). Because these models are so large and require such computational resources to train, it is common to distribute fitted model parameters in an open-source way for others to use.

To derive deep topical groupings of articles, first, we use the *distilbert-base-nli-mean-tokens* model of Reimers and Gurevych (2019) to produce a vector representation of every article. This BERT-based model is particularly suited for producing fixed-length vector representations of passages. We then compress the vectors from 768 dimensions to 5 dimensions using UMAP (McInnes et al., 2018) to increase the efficiency of the next steps, and then cluster the compressed article vectors using HDBSCAN (McInnes & Healy, 2017) to produce a hierarchical clustering, following which we extract a flat clustering by the excess-of-mass method. This technique is robust to outliers and it does not require assigning every article to one of the clusters. Our approach can be seen as an extension of work by Demszky et al. (2019) who use GloVe embeddings instead of sentence-BERT and *k*-means instead of HDBSCAN. The GloVe embeddings do not capture sentence-level information, and *k*-means does not allow for points that are un-clustered, so we consider this approach to be more flexible.

The flat clusters in 5-dimensional space cannot be visualized directly. Instead, we again apply UMAP to the data, compressing the vectors to be two-dimensional and therefore plottable on a page or computer monitor. This step does not affect the clusters; it is purely for visualization. To this point, the methodology we espouse resembles Angelov (2020), but the innovation in a *vicinato* plot is to connect information from MALLET and BERT. The BERT-based topic modeling process assigns each article to a single topic, unlike the MALLET approach in which an article reflects a distribution over topics. We may want to relate these topics to other aspects of the articles, such as their source, their year of publication, their sentiment, or the prevalence of a given MALLET-based topic within each article. To this end, we can represent each of these with a different visual modality. As shown in Fig. 4.1, we can represent BERT-based topic with color and MALLET topic loading with size in the scatter plots. We call these scatter plots *vicinato* plots, from the Italian word meaning *neighborhood* and the plots' tendency to arrange points into neighborhoods of like articles (© McCarthy et al., 2021: A. Supplement: Vicinato Plots).

Finance emerges as one of the prevalent topics that both Hong Kong– and western-based newspapers covered in relation to the episodes of protests in Hong Kong. Yet, as Figs. 4.1 and 4.2 show, compared to the breadth and depth of coverage of the other topics, finance does not emerge as particularly relevant. Western–and Hong Kong-based newspapers' use of the finance frame when covering the protests mirrors each other between 1998 and 2020, particularly in the coverage peaks of 1999, 2007, 2014, and 2019. In 2019–2020, however, the coverage of the impacts of the anti-ELAB protests on finance is more voluminous in the SCMP and the China Daily than western-based newspapers. We use BERT to achieve a more granular understanding of the *kind* of coverage that western- and Hong Kong–based newspapers achieved through the employment of the finance frame, one that the top words identified by MALLET—*cent, per cent, Hong Kong, market, property, billion, company, million, price, sale*—did not allow for.

In Fig. 4.4, the triangular collection of points on the extreme right identifies the coverage of the protests through the *Finance* frame. Their proximity to each other and relative separation from the remainder of the articles point to their content being quite different from all others. Moreover, the variation in density within the finance cluster allows us to establish a link between a specific point in time over the course of the 2019 protests, a particular episode within the protests, and the newspapers' coverage of the finance topic. Our analysis suggests that the SCMP uses the salience of economic considerations in its reporting on the protests more than the China Daily or any of the western-based newspapers. This focus on Hong Kong's financial reputation, in turn, is likely to project views about the protests that are closer to those of Beijing.

Of the 595 articles on the topic *Finance* published in 2019, 557 were published between July and December 2019, when some of the most violent civic unrest in the history of Hong Kong took place. For instance, August 2019 witnessed a five-day protesters' sit-in, starting around August 9 and ending on August 13. It brought the Hong Kong International Airport to a complete halt and ended in intense physical confrontations between the protesters and the police, which resulted in a significant number of arrests. The Hong Kong International Airport is the world's eighth busiest airport and handles around 200,000 passengers every day. The financial impacts of even a single-day shutdown could include air cargo losses for 1.44 billion US dollars and revenue losses for 3.24 million US dollars.

Qualitative content analysis and descriptive inference of a random sample of articles from the SCMP on its coverage of the incidents surrounding the five-day sit-in reveal an emphasis on the need for the protesters to reflect on the negative economic impacts of their actions, perhaps in an effort to instill calm and reassure investors about the stability and continued viability of Hong Kong as a financial hub. In fact, on August 21, 2019, the SCMP used the protest paradigm to highlight how the protests impacted the transport of gold to mainland China:

> *Hong Kong's political crisis could damage the city's leading position in the gold market (...) confrontations between the police and protesters had become increasingly violent over the summer, culminating at Hong Kong International Airport last week when hundreds of flights were cancelled. The cancellations disrupted the transport of gold arrivals into the city, including those in transit to the mainland, raising the question of whether Beijing would look for other avenues to accumulate its holdings. More importantly, the protests have fuelled worries of whether Hong Kong's role as a global financial centre in the Greater Bay Area plan will shrink. The Chinese government may be looking for other avenues as Hong Kong's biggest gold-storage facility is on the ground floor of a building in the international airport. Experts estimated that at least HK$2 billion worth of the metal had fled the city in the past week or so. In the meantime, competition is building, and could come from neighboring Shenzhen, along with Hong Kong and Macau, that are part of the Greater Bay Area development plan, and will be underpinned by the "one country, two systems" principle for the two special administrative regions (SARs) of Hong Kong and Macau.*

In the same way, on August 31, 2019, the SCMP wrote about the impact of the protests on the operations of Tiffany & Co., for which Hong Kong is the jeweler's fourth biggest market relative to total sales, after the United States, Japan, and mainland China:

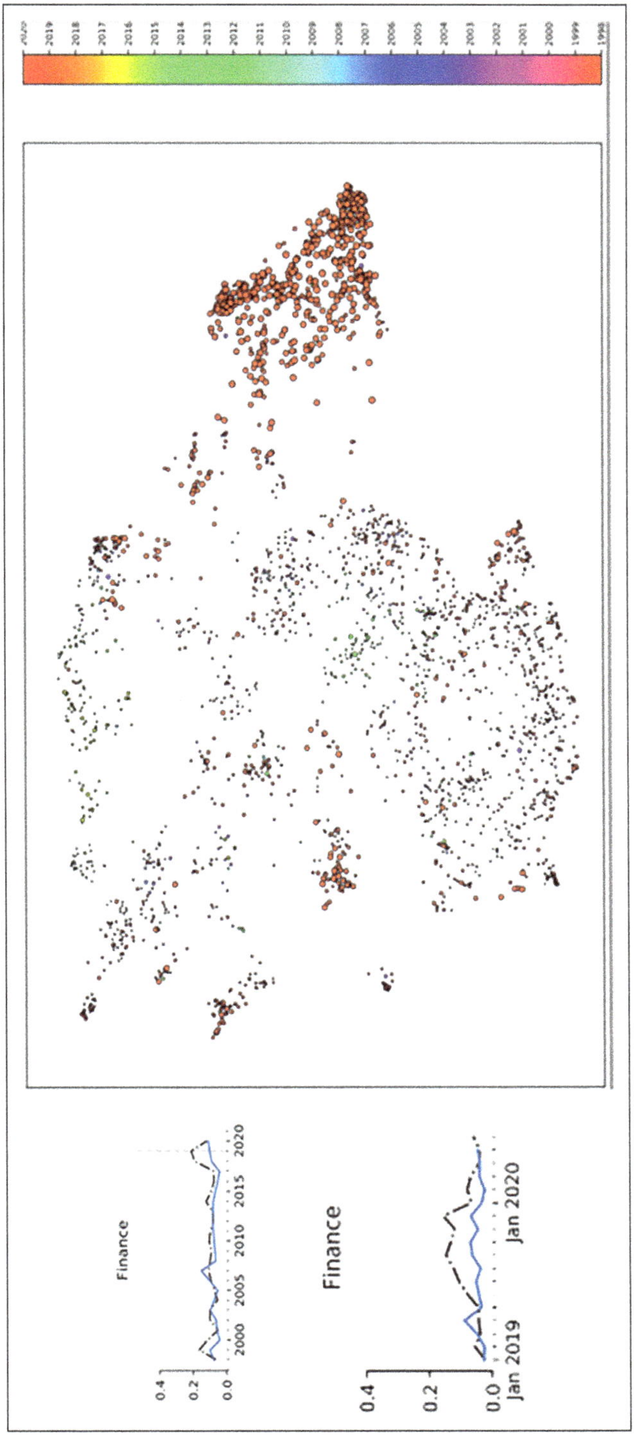

Fig. 4.4 BERT-MALLET plots for the Finance frame, 1998–2020. (Source: Authors)

American jeweller Tiffany & Co warned of the toll taken on its business by the social unrest in Hong Kong as its worldwide net sales and earnings dipped in the second quarter. Global reported sales decreased 3 percent and net earnings fell 6 percent, in part due to a significant decline in both sales attributed to Chinese and all other tourists and to business disruption in Hong Kong. "In Hong Kong, where we have 10 stores and have been presented with a unique set of challenges," chief executive Alessandro Bogliolo said on a conference call to discuss financial results for the second quarter. "Obviously, we hope for a quick and peaceful resolution to the unrest being experienced there, but in the meantime, we must acknowledge that the current situation is taking a toll on our business." The Hong Kong Retail Management Association last week said most of its members suffered a 50 percent sales drop in the first three weeks of August. Tiffany & Co's net earnings in the quarter declined 6 per cent to US$136 million from US$145 million in the previous year. Worldwide net sales in the second quarter fell 3 per cent to US$1.04 billion from US$1.07 billion in the previous year. Net sales in the Asia-Pacific fell 1 per cent to US$298 million, reflecting strong growth on the mainland, softness in Hong Kong and a mixed performance in other markets in the Asia-Pacific region, the company said.

In an effort to emphasize Hong Kong's macroeconomic and financial stability, on August 31, 2019, the SCMP wrote about the financial health of the Exchange Fund, the financial mechanisms that the Hong Kong government can use to defend the Hong Kong dollar[12]:

Hong Kong's financial system is holding up in the face of the city's public unrest, with the Exchange Fund reporting an increase for July and only a small amount of capital flowing out in the month. The size of the Exchange Fund – used by the government to defend the currency – grew by 0.02 per cent, or HK$700 million, to HK$4.138 trillion at the end of July, bolstering the government's defences against hedge funds that are eyeing a chance to short-sell the currency amid slower economic growth and the year-long US-China trade war. The financial system's aggregate balance, an indicator of banking liquidity, dipped by 0.06 per cent in July to HK$54.24 billion from a month earlier, according to Hong Kong Monetary Authority (HKMA) data. The July balance declined by 50 per cent from last year, as the authority used money in the Exchange Fund to keep the currency's peg within a trading band against the US dollar. Total deposits in the city's financial institutions, meanwhile, shrank in July by HK$4.39 billion, or 0.03 per cent, to HK$13.603 trillion, the data showed. The HKMA has sufficient assets in the Exchange Fund to defend the exchange rate of the

[12] On September 24, 1983, months of consumer and investor anxiety over the rapid depreciation of the Hong Kong dollar, coupled with concern over Chinese and British negotiations about the city's return to mainland rule, culminated in the Black Saturday crisis. Panic selling of the local currency drove its value to an all-time low (of 9.6 per US dollar, down from 6.5 per US dollar) at the start of the year, under the floating exchange rate system. Faced with public unrest and wavering confidence in Hong Kong's banks, Financial Secretary John Bremridge announced the introduction of a linked exchange system on October 17, 1983, which pegged the currency to the US dollar at a fixed rate. The Hong Kong dollar was originally set at a rate of 7.8 per US dollar; though since 2005, it has been allowed to trade between 7.75 and 7.85 per US dollar. When the Hong Kong currency hits the low end of the band, the Hong Kong Monetary Authority, the city's de facto central bank, is bound to start buying up the currency to boost its value. The peg's introduction was an effort to re-establish confidence among citizens, investors, and corporations, while also signaling that the Hong Kong financial system was distinct from that of mainland China. The peg's fixed exchange rate has allowed Hong Kong to strengthen its status as an international financial center, and withstand the stock market crash in 1987, the Asian financial crisis in 1998, the severe acute respiratory syndrome outbreak in 2003, and the global financial crisis in 2008. https://www.hkma.gov.hk/eng/news-and-media/insight/1999/11/19991104/

Hong Kong dollar, which has remained stable in recent months. (…) "There has been a lot of speculation about people moving their money to other markets, but the data shows a massive outflow is not happening.

Then, there are the 107 articles that the SCMP published in October 2019, which is the month that saw some of the most violent protests, including those on October 1, China National Day, which morphed into a whole day of violence, fires, vandalism, the throwing of Molotov cocktails, and the shooting of a teenager. On October 28, 2019, the SCMP wrote about the cost of the October protests in terms of insurance claims:

Insurance claims related to arson, vandalism and loss of business because of the anti-government protests that have taken place since June may have reached nearly HK\$600 million so far, marking the third-largest amount in Hong Kong's history. In the ongoing social unrest, protesters have targeted rail operator MTR Corporation, the local branches of mainland banks such as Bank of China and Industrial and Commercial Bank of China, as well as businesses with mainland links or whose owners support Beijing. The MTR Corp alone may seek HK\$100 million as it has borne the brunt of protesters' ire, with demonstrators setting fire to the entrances of almost all its stations and vandalising its property (…) and a further HK\$400 million of claims related to losses over business interruption at hotels, shops and banks whose operations had been affected because of property damage or other issues.

In November 2019, the months during which protests transformed Hong Kong's universities into "battlegrounds",[13] some 80 articles were published on the economic impacts of nine months of protests and the costs associated with those events. In fact, on November 29, the SCMP wrote:

Troubled Hong Kong Airlines (HKA) yesterday said it could not afford to pay almost half of its staff their salaries for November on time, delaying the payments until the first week of December. In an internal note, the HNA-backed carrier's human resources department blamed the anti-government protests, now in their sixth month, for its inability to pay employees on time. "Hong Kong Airlines' business has been severely affected by the social unrest and sustained weak travel demand," the memo said. "With November being a low travel season as well, our revenue has been reduced significantly, affecting our payroll for the month." The airline said its cabin crew and overseas staff would be paid on time, but all other staff would get paid on December 6. About 1,600 employees will be affected, close to 45 per cent of the carrier's 3,560 employees. The financial position of Hong Kong's third largest airline has been so weak the government had to intervene in its business earlier this month, demanding urgent improvements and placing it under more public scrutiny. The Air Licensing Transport Authority – a statutory body with the power to shut down carriers and approve new ones – warned in late October it would impose measures if HKA's financial situation did not improve. (…) Carriers, such as Cathay Pacific, have been able to offset the downturn by relying more on transit passengers, who bypass Hong Kong, and offering cheap fares. "We understand this arrangement may cause you inconvenience and sincerely apologise for it," HKA said in its memo to staff.

The day after, on November 30, the SCMP wrote:

Hong Kong police lift cordon around polytechnic university to end stand-off that began almost two weeks ago. A university caught in the crossfire between radical protesters and

[13] The South China Morning Post, November 28, 2019.

police will face a substantial bill and take up to half a year to repair, its president said yesterday. Teng Jin-guang, president of Polytechnic University, spoke as a 13-day police siege of the campus came to an end. The term has been suspended and vast damage inflicted on the university's facilities and laboratories. As soon as police left the campus they had besieged since November 17, nearby roads were reopened, while the campus was guarded by security personnel hired by the university. The police withdrawal came a day after they went in to search for evidence and remove hazardous items. A total of 3,989 petrol bombs, 1,339 pieces of explosives and 601 bottles of corrosive liquid had been found, alongside 573 seized items that were classified as weapons, the force said. The weapons included hammers, air guns, 28 bows and about 200 arrows, and 12 giant catapults used to launch bricks. More than 1,000 radical protesters and their supporters occupied the campus a fortnight ago, and engaged in fierce battles with police on November 17. Thel cost was as yet unknown, he said, as they needed to hire professionals to provide an estimate. The government pulled about HK$2 billion in funding proposals to the Legislative Council to build medical and library facilities at three universities, including PolyU, this month after pro-establishment lawmakers expressed dismay that varsity management failed to control their institutions, which had become battlefields in the protests.

Overall, the findings from the BERT *Vicinato* plots on *Finance* and the excerpts discussed in the previous pages point to the SCMP's extensive use of rhetorical tactics. Most prominent among these is the protest paradigm. The SCMP uses it to manage the protests' narrative, pushing toward two goals in parallel. It keeps international readers focused on the implications that civic unrest may have on Hong Kong's role as both China's financial gateway and financial firewall. At the same time, it portrays the protests as radical in their goals and extreme in their tactics, presenting the protesters as a group apart from the overwhelming majority of Hong Kong's citizens. It is likely that the SCMP hoped to separate and downplay the reality of Hong Kong as the city where disruption and social unrest was happening, while reinforcing that of a city with one of the most open economies in the world, one which guaranteed financial freedoms that remain unavailable in mainland China, in an effort to stay appealing to investors worldwide.

4.3 The Lexicon Used to Portray the Hong Kong Protests

Having categorized salient themes in the articles, we now turn to the use of specific, protest-relevant keywords.[14] Word frequency exposes obvious discrepancies in word choice and word usage. A lack of event-related keywords in contemporaneous articles from different newspapers may signal the omission of events in some of them. Each source will have some degree of variation in keyword counts. As an author's voice accounts for some mismatch in frequency, but not all, the challenge

[14] For the purpose of this research, the term *keyword* is used in the information retrieval rather than the corpus linguistic sense, meaning a term that is statistically characteristic in a text. See also Douglas Biber and Randi Reppen (Eds.). (2015). *The Cambridge Handbook of English Corpus Linguistics*. Cambridge: Cambridge University Press, pp. 90–105.

to determine the reasons the emerging distribution of keyword counts remains a formidable one.

We first test for whether there are important differences in the frequencies of 19 protest-related keywords: *confront*, *confrontation*, *crackdown*, *democracy*, *freedom*, *freedom of speech*, *independence*, *occupation*, *protest*, *protests*, *resistance*, *rights*, *riot*, *rule of law*, *severe*, *tension*, *terrorism*, *terrorist*, *unrest*. For one keyword at a time, we perform the following steps: (i) split the corpus in two by some categorical attribute; (ii) obtain the keyword's frequency in each article of both corpora; and then (iii) apply a statistical test to establish whether our categorical variable—*in our case the location of the article's publisher*—is associated with a variation in frequency. As our corpus shows a non-parametric distribution, we apply Mann–Whitney U, splitting by newspaper source and using the Holm–Bonferroni correction with significance level of $\alpha = 0.01$, to understand whether any of the 19 keywords of interest has statistically significant differences in usage.

The Mann–Whitney U shows that every word has statistically significant differences in usage except *severe*. The same test, splitting by before and after June 2019, shows statistically significant differences only for five (out of the 19) keywords: *protests*, *unrest*, *rights*, *rule of law*, and *democracy*. For the Friedman's test with four categories—that is "West before June"; "West after June"; "Hong Kong before June"; and "Hong Kong after June"—no keyword showed statistically significant differences.

4.3.1 Democracy and Freedom

A count for the words *democracy* and *freedom* reveals that, with the exception of 2019–2020, the SCMP and the China Daily have used these two terms less often than western-based newspapers.

In fact, between 1998 and 2020, *freedom* appears 70 times in the SCMP and the China Daily and 492 in western-based newspapers; *democracy* appears 107 in Hong Kong–based newspapers and 242 times in western-based newspapers. In 2014, *freedom* appears only 18 times in Hong Kong–based newspapers and 127 times in western-based ones, whereas *democracy* appears 34 times more in western–based than Hong Kong–based newspapers (i.e., 416: 12). These trends are reversed in 2019–2020, when *freedom* appears 755 times in the SCMP and the China Daily and 365 in western-based newspapers. *Democracy* appears 668 times in Hong Kong–based newspapers and 217 times in western-based ones. However, as shown in Fig. 4.5, the frequencies of use of *democracy* and *freedom* are, overall, lower in Hong Kong–based newspapers than that found in western–based newspapers. Moreover, western-based newspapers used *democracy* and *freedom* prevalently as a noun, whereas Hong Kong-based newspapers tend to use both terms more often as qualifiers rather than as nouns.

The difference in frequencies may be partially rooted in the type of articles that the newspapers publish. For instance, in 2019–2020, western-based newspapers

Democracy

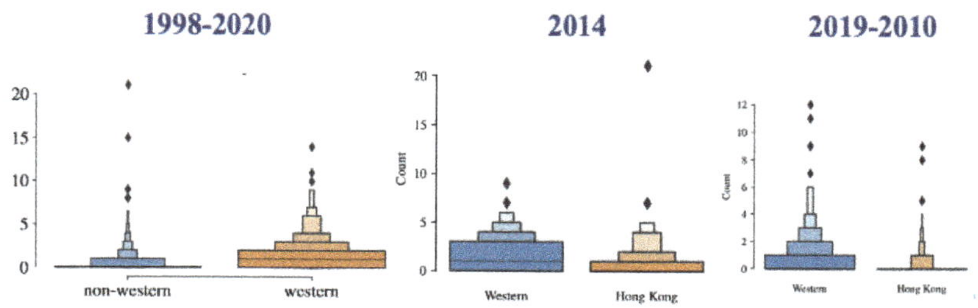

	Western-based newspapers	Hong Kong-based newspapers
1998-2020	875/793 = 1.103	787/ 3729 = 0.211
2014	416/236 = 1.762	12/131 = 0.091
2019-2020	217/390 = 0.556	668/3009 = 0.222

Freedom

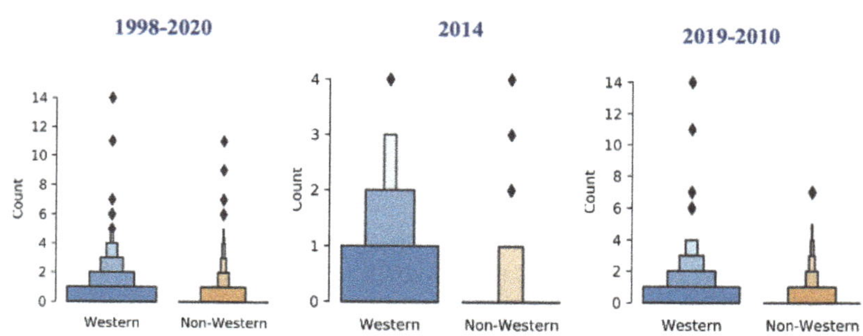

	Western-based newspapers	Hong Kong-based newspapers
1998-2020	575/793 = 0.725	843/ 3729 = 0.221
2014	127/236 = 0.538	18/131 = 0.131
2019-2020	365/390 = 0.936	755/3009 = 0.251

Fig. 4.5 Quantile plot of democracy and freedom counts per article, by newspaper source. (Source: Authors)

tended to cast citizens' dissent over ELAB as a citizens' fight for democracy and the freedoms that come with it, or resistance against the authoritarian tightening that Hong Kong has been experiencing following the 1997 handover. This narrative may require a more frequent use and/or discussion of democracy and freedom as *concepts* and *values*, as in the October 27, 2019 NYT article which quotes, "*We just don't want to become like those Chinese who have become accustomed to living without freedom*"; the June 17, 2019 FT article quoting Taiwan's President Tsai Ing-wen's reaction to the Hong Kong government's response to a peaceful protest "*When the freedom of the people of Hong Kong is facing a retreat under the trap of 'one country, two systems' set by China, we should resolutely guard the democracy and freedom of Taiwan*"; and the WSJ reporting on May 28, 2020 that "*mass crowds then took to the streets to call for greater democracy and defend Hong Kong's relative autonomy from China.*"

On the other hand, the SCMP and the China Daily tended to focus their discourse narrowly on the details of the protests rather than on their meaning. For instance, the SCMP article of August 9, 2019 reported, "*If this was a revolution, Sin was the archetypal freedom fighter*"; and the China Daily argued on September 24, 2019 that "*some in the West have even called the insurrectionists 'pro-democracy fighters' when the truth is that the demonstrators have thrown SAR residents' daily life out of gear and harmed their livelihoods. It is ironical that the 'pro-democracy' demonstrators claim to be protecting universal values despite doing exactly the opposite: breaking the law.*" This narrative lends itself well to *democracy* and *freedom* used sparingly and as qualifiers across the large number of articles published.

4.3.2 Protests

While Hong Kong protest politics can be traced back to the late 1960s, when it became an important undercurrent in the local political scene (Lam, 2004), what protests include remains broad and not clearly defined. Before and just after the 1997 handover, *protest*s mainly indicated *demonstrations* and *rallies*. Even though political parties, trade unions and NGOs organized protests on a daily basis (Cheng, 2016), protests were, generally, limited to one or several dozen people, some of whom could be recruited as temporary demonstrators which, at times, made protests contrived, contradicting the (worldwide) impression that they were genuine or spontaneous. Protests grew in frequency and size in the early 2000s as citizens' perception of democratic backsliding increased, with large rallies becoming an integral part of the protest scene and attracting tens to hundreds of thousands of participants.[15] Records from the Hong Kong Security Bureau and LegCo show that between July 1997 and September 2012, under the Public Order Ordinance,[16] the

[15] See pages 4–6.

[16] https://www.elegislation.gov.hk/hk/cap245

Police approved 51,915 applications for *legal procession*, which refers to a public meeting of more than 50 people or a public procession of more than 30 people. Moreover, data also suggest that 2003, 2006–2007, and 2012 were "critical junctures at which the number of collective actions increased rapidly; and since then, the percentage change in legal procession –year-to-year– emerges as highly correlated with the timing of the protests themselves" (Cheng, 2016: 389).

Its familiarity and persistent nebulousness make *protest* a "contentious term" (Tarrow, 2013: 267–274), whose use in the printed media could either amplify and legitimize or marginalize and delegitimize episodes of civic unrest, and in doing so shape the public's perception of, and support for, such events (Gamson & Wolfsfeld, 1993). For instance, the July 1 protests earned a reputation for being peaceful, rational, and non-violent, with growing numbers of protesters marching on 15 consecutive years, with only a few dozen assaults and not a single robbery. In contrast, the other episodes of protest whose news coverage is included in the *Hong Kong Protest News Dataset* involved occupations, sieges, hunger strikes, or blockades to which the police reacted by repeatedly using violence against the protesters (Ibrahim & Lam, 2020).

The frequency with which the terms *protests*, *marches*, *rallies,* and *riots* appear in all articles, both in their plain count, any-form frequency, and corresponding densities help unpack how Hong Kong– and western-based newspapers covered the protests between 1998 and 2020. Figure 4.6 shows that, over the 22–year timeline of our research, neither all 3729 articles by the SCMP and the China Daily, nor the 793 articles published by western-based newspapers include the word *protests* or some form of it. Figure 4.7, however, shows that in the case of the 2019 anti-ELAB protests, all 390 articles from western-based newspapers include the word *protests* or some form of it, whereas not all articles from SCMP and the China Daily do. In fact, out of 3009 articles, 2932 used *protests* or a form of it. Of the remainder, 14 used a form of *riot*, 29 used a form of *march*, and 34 used a form of *rally*.

Finally, Fig. 4.8 shows that in the case of the 2014 Occupy Central protests, all 131 articles from the SCMP and the China Daily include the word *protests* or some form of it, whereas not all articles from western–based newspapers do. This suggests a SCMP's and China Daily's continued emphasis on labeling these as protests, with all the implications that the word carries. By contrast, when western newspapers discuss the same incidents, they show a greater diversity in the particular lexicon that they use—even though, as we show, their general rhetorical tactic of the protest paradigm remains steady.

Our research found that, in their use of the terms *protest*, *march*, *rally*, and *riot*, the SCMP and the China Daily tend to delegitimize and marginalize both the protests and the protesters . Delegitimization and marginalization take various forms within the news, involving both microlevel (e.g., physical composition; general elements of the story itself) and macrolevel (e.g., overall tone of the story; main framing used throughout) factors, and are consistent with McLeod and Hertog's "mechanisms of social control in media coverage of social protest" (1999: 305). Qualitative content analysis conducted on a random sample of 25% of the articles from our corpus shows that in the article contexts within which the SCMP and the China Daily prefer to embed the

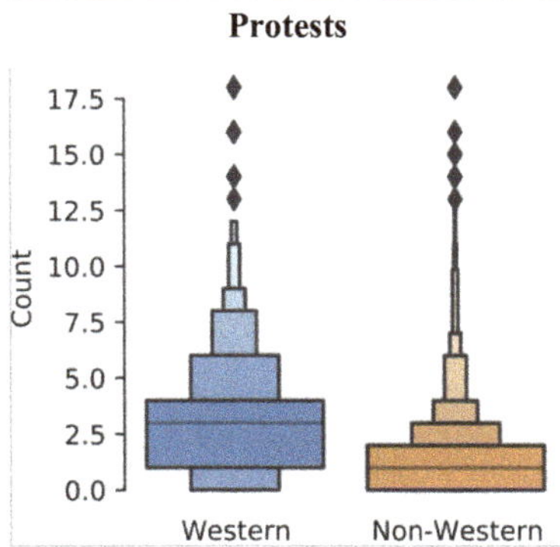

Newspaper source	Word	Frequency	Any Form Frequency	Density	Any form Density
Western- based newspapers (793 articles)	Protests	702	782	0.8852	0.9861
	Rallies	113	273	0.1425	0.3443
	Marches	55	291	0.0694	0.3670
	Riots	36	220	0.0454	0.2774
Hong Kong- based newspapers (3729 articles)	Protests	2863	3362	0.7678	0.9016
	Rallies	264	790	0.0708	0.2119
	Marches	135	827	0.0362	0.2218
	Riots	127	759	0.0341	0.2035

Fig. 4.6 Quantile plot of protests counts per article, by newspapers source in 1998–2020. (Source: Authors)

terms *protest*, *march*, *rally*, and *riot* privilege lawlessness and police confrontation, discussion of "protest as performance" (McFarlane and Hay, 2003: 218) with coverage "highlighting spectacle and the theatrical elements of a protest" (Dardis, 2006: 120). Over time, and especially starting in 2014, the SCMP and the China Daily also began to discuss the protests in terms of "treason and/or anarchy" (Dardis, 2006: 121), or through historical comparison with episodes of civic unrest or protest groups that may not have been seen favorably among Hongkongers (Hackett & Zhao, 1994) with the intent to delegitimize protesters and thereby the utility and value of protests in general (McLeod & Detenber, 1999).

4.4 Differences in *How* Hong Kong – And Western-Based Newspapers Portray the Protests

4.4.1 Sentiment Analysis

The tone that a newspaper espouses when covering protests can be indicative of its attitudes towards them. We therefore apply computational sentiment analysis to measures the tone and connotations of articles. While it is common to use

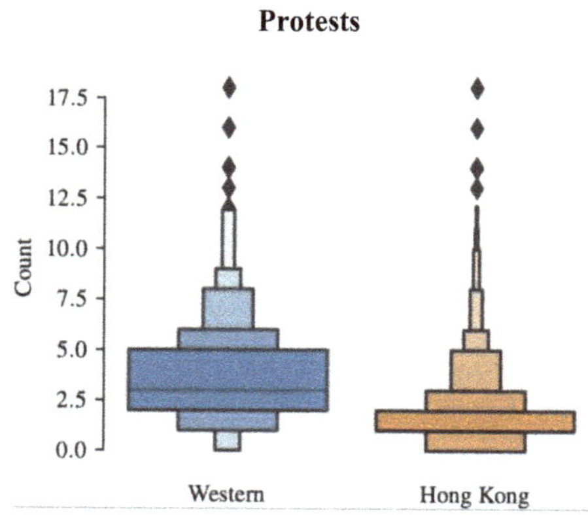

Newspaper source	Word	Frequency	Any form frequency	Density	Any form density
Western-based newspapers (390 articles)	Protests	376	390	0.9641	1
	Rallies	74	168	0.1897	0.4307
	Marches	39	174	0.1	0.4461
	Riots	27	168	0.0692	0.4307
Hong Kong-based newspapers (3009 articles)	Protests	2526	2824	0.8394	0.9385
	Rallies	222	610	0.0737	0.2027
	Marches	119	636	0.0395	0.2113
	Riots	120	691	0.0398	0.2296

Fig. 4.7 Quantile plot of protests counts per article, by newspapers source in 2019–2020. (Source: Authors)

hand-crafted sentiment (valency) lexica (Mohammad, 2018), they are necessarily incomplete (see §4.1) and sentiment depend on more than lexicon choice; it is crucial to consider how words are used in context. We, therefore, selected a technique that is robust to the specific words that are chosen. We chose a BERT-based model to classify a given sentence as positive or negative because of its near state-of-the-art sentiment classification abilities. We treat sentiment as a binary attribute (+, −)[17] and use a probabilistic classifier trained on the Stanford Sentiment Treebank (SST-2; Socher et al., 2013). The logistic regression model uses DistilBERT (Sanh et al., 2019) for feature extraction from text; DistilBERT has previously been used for sentiment analysis of product reviews (Büyüköz et al., 2020). We split each article into sentences, then classify each sentence. An article's sentiment is taken as the average sentiment over all of its sentences. Sentiment score may provide evidence of stylometric differences between newspapers sources, which together with the analysis of lexical usage and topic model.

We corroborate the findings of a more negative tone in the SCMP and the China Daily by using computational sentiment analysis, which measures the tone and

[17] There is merit to including a third 'it's complicated' class (Kenyon-Dean et al., 2018).

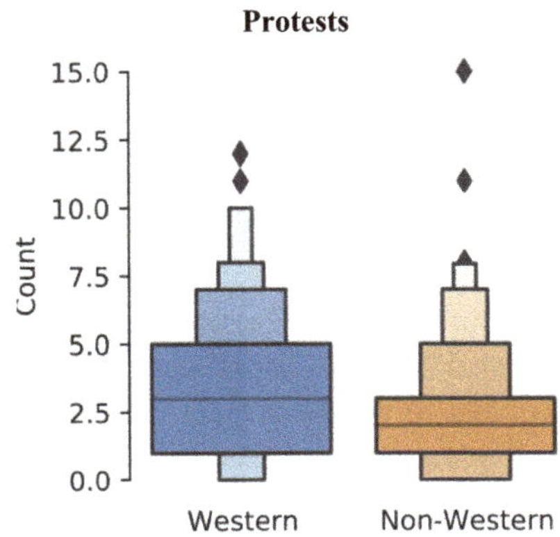

Newspaper source	Word	Frequency	Any form frequency	Density	Any form density
Western-based newspapers (236 articles)	Protests	217	234	0.9195	0.9914
	Rallies	23	58	0.0975	0.2458
	Marches	8	37	0.0339	0.1568
	Riots	4	40	0.0169	0.1695
Hong Kong-based newspapers (131 articles)	Protests	108	131	0.8244	1
	Rallies	5	19	0.0382	0.1450
	Marches	2	15	0.0152	0.1145
	Riots	4	5	0.0305	0.0382

Fig. 4.8 Quantile plot of protests counts per article, by newspapers source in 2014. (Source: Authors)

connotations of articles. Between 1998 and 2020, Hong Kong–based articles' average positivity is around 36.9%, which is slightly lower than the 38.1% of western–based articles. The more negative sentiment of the articles published in the SCMP in particular leverages the relevance and usefulness of the protest paradigm in discussing civic unrest in Hong Kong. On the other hand, the slightly more positive sentiment present in the western–based coverage supports that the western news sources use of the protest paradigm in a different, facilitating capacity: they paint violent protests as the most effective means for protesters to be heard (McCluskey et al., 2009).

Our analysis, however, shows that there is wide variation across sources. At 31.3% and 31.5% the SCMP and The Times, in fact, emerge as the newspapers with the most negative tone overall, even though the SCMP published the most articles on the Hong Kong protests, whereas the Times rarely publishes articles about the protests. Both The Guardian, at 32.9%, and The Financial Times, at 33.9%, also rank low in positivity, which makes UK-based newspapers the more negative about Hong Kong protests among western-based newspapers. This finding might be seen as the legacy of the UK's mixed feelings regarding Hong Kong's handover to China, in spite of Prime Minister Thatcher's 1984 statement that "We have got an agreement which is acceptable overwhelmingly to the people of Hong Kong. That agreement will extend into 50 years beyond 1997. I feel we have done a good job for the people of Hong Kong."[18] US-based newspapers average a positivity score of 36%, with the NYT articles being almost imperceptibly more positive than those of the WSJ (i.e., 36.3% vs 36.1%) and WaPo (i.e., 36.3% vs 36.0%). At 40%, the China Daily has the most positive tone among both Hong Kong–and western–based newspapers. Moreover, it is worth noting that average positivity of the SCMP and China Daily articles remains lower than that of western-based newspapers articles in 2014 (i.e., 33.2% vs 35.7%), and also in 2019–2020 (i.e., 31.4% vs 32.9%). Finally, these discoveries boost those related to non-rhetorical tactics as discussed in Chap. 3, particularly the timing and volume of coverage by both Hong Kong- and western-based newspapers.

4.4.2 Comparing Embedding Neighborhoods

While our sentiment score provides evidence of stylometric differences between newspapers sources, an investigation of word embedding neighborhoods furthers our understanding of *how* words are used differently between the SCMP, the China Daily, and western–based newspapers, and *how* the contexts of protest-related keywords differ across news sources.

Diachronic shifts in the understanding of a word are reflected in changes in the word's usage. Corpus linguistics recognizes this in shifts in collocational preferences: the word is used in a new pattern of sentential context as its meaning evolves. A methodological successor of this is the use of a smoothed notion of collocation based on word embeddings. There, the semantic shift manifests as change in the word's neighbors in an embedding space (Hamilton et al., 2016; Gonen et al., 2020). For instance, Hamilton et al. (2016) used these to find a shift in the word *broadcast* from agricultural to television contexts between the 1850s and 1900s. The same procedure can identify differences between words' usage when separated by something other than time. A word embedding model seeks to assign similar vectors (measured by dot product) to words in similar contexts, and different vectors to words in different contexts. If the usage of a word changes, then this should be reflected in changes to the word's context and consequent changes in the word's embedding. We both replicate and extend the *difference-in-usage model* of Gonen et al. (2020), which measures how the contexts of words differ.

1. Partition the corpus C into C_a and $C_{\bar{a}}$ based on the attribute of interest a.[19]
2. Fit separate word embedding models for each partition: M_a and $M_{\bar{a}}$.
3. Select a keyword w of interest.

[18] https://www.npr.org/2019/07/01/737761290/looking-back-22-years-to-the-handover-of-hong-kong-from-britain-to-china

[19] For instance, whether the article is written by the western or the Hong Kong press.

4. Obtain the set of nearest neighbors $NN_a(w)$ and $NN_{\bar{a}}(w)$ of w according to each of M_a and $M_{\bar{a}}$.[20]
5. Score the usage-change of w as the size of the intersection, $\mathrm{NN}_a(w) \cap \mathrm{NN}_{\bar{a}}(w)$.

After this process, if w is used differently based on the presence or absence of the attribute, we expect its score to be quite small. Words whose usage does not depend on the attribute will have similar neighborhoods in each split. To extend the work of Gonen et al. (2020), we contextualize the similarity score of a given word against a reference set. Considering all words that occur at least 100 times, in which percentile does word w's similarity score fall? We find this to be more meaningful than the raw similarity score.

Table 4.3 shows the results of *how* words are used differently between the SCMP, the China Daily, and western– based newspapers, and *how* the contexts of protest-related keywords differ across news sources between 1998 and 2020. Of relevance for our analysis is the lexical usage of the words *riot* (98th percentile), *protest* (88th percentile), *occupation* (80th percentile), *confrontation* (70th percentile), and *tensions* (59th percentile). A visual inspection of the term's nearest neighbors for the western-based model suggests the prevalence of descriptive lexicon as in the case of *scene, clearance, dispersal, crowds* for the word *riot*; *sit-ins, rally, campaign* for the word *protest*; or *dispute, turmoil, uncertainty* for the word *tensions*. In contrast, the nearest neighbors in the model for the SCMP and China Daily relate to adversarial behavior as in the case of *fired, barricades, pepper, teargas* for the word *riot; break, standoff, storm, chaotic, dislodge* for the word *confrontation*. These trends are evidence of the SCMP's and the China Daily's choice of taking advantage of the protest paradigm to "to question the legitimacy of the protests or the protest groups, to marginalize the protests accentuating the deviance of the protesters from the mainstream public, and to demonize the protests by exaggerating the potential threat of a protest group" (McLeod & Hertog, 1999: 311).

In the lexical usage for the 2014 Occupy Central protests and the 2019–2020 anti-ELAB protests, we detect trends in certain keywords between the SCMP, the China Daily and western-based newspapers that are consistent with those found for the coverage of protests between 1998 and 2020 (see Table 4.3). In the case of the 2014 Occupy Central protests, this is the case of *occupation* (75th percentile), *protest* (61st percentile), *confrontation* (53rd percentile), whereas in the case of 2019–2020 anti-ELAB protests, similar are found in the lexical usage of *protests* (66th percentile) and *tensions* (63rd percentile). The consistent prevalence of a neutral or descriptive lexicon for the western-based models, the recurrency of an adversarial behavior lexicon for the Hong Kong–based model are likely to be linked to the specific characteristics of the various episodes of protests. On the other hand, they may also be explained by Hong Kong media's "norms of political correctness" (Lee, 2007a: 137) vis-à-vis Beijing, or the "strategic rituals" (Lee, 2007b: 439) which Hong Kong newspapers have established to counter Beijing's "strategic ambiguity"

[20] Following the recommendation of Wendlandt et al. (2018) and Gonen et al. (2020), we use 1000 nearest neighbors.

Table 4.3 Semantic divergence, in keywords between the SCMP, China Daily and western-based newspapers

1998–2020	
SCMP and China Daily	**Western-based newspapers**
Riot (98th percentile)	
Fired, spray, barricades, officers, pepper, station, rubber, cocktail, firing, teargas	Mob, rampage, mobs, siege, scene, clearance, dispersal, crowds, clash, radicals
Protest (88th percentile)	
Activities, peaceful, rally, mass, organizers, demonstrations, street, occupied, admiralty, rally	Demonstrations, sit-ins, rally, demonstration, campaign, rallies, march, movement, sit-in, protest
Occupation (80th percentile)	
Denounce, supporters, peacefully, confrontation, join, occupying, radical, momentum, peaceful, anti-government	Mayhem, rallies, demonstrations, demonstration, marches, sit-ins, outburst, bloody, 79-day, scene
Confrontation (79th percentile)	
Peacefully, break, dramatically, preparing, standoff, storm, driving, demonstrate, chaotic, dislodge	Turning, stand-off, mayhem, resorting, confrontations, extreme, resorted, quickly, disruptive, chaotic
Tensions (59th percentile)	
Plunged, duel, population, impatience, marks, takeover, mark, recession, curb, annual	Tension, dispute, turmoil, US-China, war, heightened, uncertainty, blow, protracted, dispute
2019–2020	
SCMP and China Daily	**Western-based newspapers**
Riot (99th percentile)	
Fired, rubber, bullets, rounds, pepper, cannon, officers, demonstrators, canisters, firing	Mob, scene, mobs, clearance, arson, bomb, dispersal, projectile, armed, rampage
Protest (91st percentile)	
Demonstrations, began, streets, mass, contrasts, violent, hundreds, peaceful, umbrella, movement	Rallies, campaign, demonstrations, demonstration, rally, mayhem, movement, chaos, strike, demonstrators
Confrontation (77th percentile)	
Attack, front-line, tactics, guns, nearby, videos, shooting, nonviolent, vehicle, track	Confrontations, scenes, flashpoints, engaged, mayhem, shocking, chaotic, protracted, ongoing
Tensions (64th percentile)	
Rebuke, ruled, communism, steps, reduced, state-owned, capital, its, argued, closer	US-China, tension, uncertainty, war, dispute, turmoil, heightened, amid, protracted, ongoing
Unrest (63rd percentile)	
Signaled, direct, fueling, wenlou, constitution, celebrated, 2014, fears, requiring, turmoil	Turmoil, tensions, crisis, events, strife, demonstrations, chaos, instability, tensions, contradictions

(continued)

Table 4.3 (continued)

2014	
SCMP and China Daily	**Western-based newspapers**
Occupation (75th percentile)	
Join, started, even, protesting, threat, thought, umbrella, planning, probably, revolution	A, court, support, work, admiralty, go, even, legal, protest, they
Protest (61st percentile)	
Movement, main, pro-democracy, student, peace, group, district, site, admiralty, love	Court, admiralty, even, a, pan-democrats, occupation, social, three, ?, way
Confrontation (53rd percentile)	
Scene, losing, showing, despite, grew, avoid, business, families, works, demonstrations	Line, lai, came, much, wong, democratic, member, sit-ins, democracy, still
Tensions (24th percentile)	
Became, questions, laws, prevent, little, half, winning, helped, closely, internal	Participants, views, rights, meant, yesterday, month, also, city, protesters, students
Riot (20th percentile)	
Attacks, spread, numbers, injunctions, sit-ins, flagging, watching, sleeping, seven, empowerment	Well, number, we, percent, dialogue, council, still, traffic, past, financial

Source: Authors

(Cheung, 2003: 231) and ensuing self-censorship, or by *cultural co-orientation* that resulted from Hong Kong journalists shifting their views to be closer to China's official views.

4.4.3 Does Coverage Differ Before and After the Outbreak of Protests in June 2019?

Our research found myriad differences in the use of both rhetorical and non-rhetorical tactics by Hong Kong– and western-based as they reported on protests between 1998 and 2020. We hypothesize *whether there are differences in these differences over time* and use the 2019–2020 anti-ELAB protest as a case study.

Statistical analysis lets us compare the means of a continuous response variable, modulated by two categorical explanatory variables; in particular, we choose Friedman's test. We use the Holm–Bonferroni correction to mitigate false discovery. In our case, the explanatory variables are the source (western/HK-based newspapers) and the date: was the article published before or after July 1, 2019? In the case of *unrest*, *democracy*, *rights*, *crackdown*, and *protest* our analysis found significant differences in the way these terms were used in newspapers before and after July 1, 2019. For the Friedman's test with four categories (western-based newspapers, Hong Kong–based newspapers) x (before, after), no keyword showed significant differences. These results suggest that any already existing biases regarding citizens' protesting and exercising their right to free speech were not discernibly altered by the onset of the anti-ELAB protests.

In our analysis, we sought to quantify the degree to which the introduction of ELAB acted as a pivotal moment in how newspapers portray the Hong Kong protests and found that June 2019 emerges as a turning point. After this, the meaning of several keywords shifts for at least the remainder of 2019. We split the corpus into "pre-June 30th, 2019" and "post-June 30th, 2019" to investigate whether the way in which Hong Kong– and western-based newspapers portrayed episodes of civic unrest differently following the protests and demonstrations that took place over the month of June 2019. Neighborhood shift analysis revealed significantly low scores for *resistance*, *severe*, *riots*, *confront*, *confrontation*, and *terrorism*, which suggests that the context and/or meaning for these words changes from early to late 2019, regardless of whether Hong Kong– or western-based news sources are considered. For instance, in the first half of 2019, neighbors for *riots* include terms like *actions*, *open*, *engage*, and *taken*, which are not charged, and in the context of either a reporting or an opinion piece descriptively inform readers. However, in the second half of 2019, the nature of neighboring terms for *riots* changes to include more polarizing terms such as *violent*, *escalated*, *destructive*, *triggered*, *anti-government*, and *sparked*. Similarly, pre-July 2019, neighbors for *terrorism* include, among others, terms like *covered*, *lawyers*, and *negative*. Post-June 2019, neighboring words become politically charged, and include *criminals*, *destructive*, *extreme*, *lawless*, *punishing*, and *barbaric*.

The findings of our analysis confirm that June 2019 was a pivotal moment in the context of the 2019–2020 Hong Kong protests. First, protests escalated exponentially during the month of June compared to earlier in the year, starting on Sunday, June 9, when an estimated one million people marched to the government headquarters to protest against the proposed bill. This was largely a peaceful rally, though some small skirmishes broke out, and their relevance was largely amplified in the SCMP and China Daily coverage of the event. Three days later, on Wednesday, June 12, a large protest march took place. It developed into the worst violence Hong Kong had witnessed in decades, with the police resorting to the use of tear gas and firing rubber bullets. Then, on Friday, June 14, Hongkongers staged a *Mothers' protest*[21] against the Police's use of violence on June 12, 2019. On Sunday, June 16, an estimated two million people took the streets demanding that ELAB be withdrawn—not just for its discussion in LegCo to be indefinitely delayed, as announced by Chief Executive Lam on June 15—and that Chief Executive Lam resign. Then, on Friday, June 21, student protesters blocked roads in the Admiralty, and besieged the Police Headquarters for 15 h. The Commissioner of Police's decision to publicly call the events of June 21 *riots*—which in the context of Hong Kong's law carries a maximum penalty of ten years imprisonment—as well Chief Executive Lam's

[21] The South China Morning Post, June 18, 2019.

Table 4.4 Neighboring terms for the word riot in the SCMP and the China Daily for 1998–2020, 2014, and 2019–2020

1998–020	2014	2019–2020
Riot (98th percentile) fired, spray, barricades, officers, pepper, station, rubber, cocktails, firing, teargas	**Riot (20th percentile)** batons, fired, shield, canisters, umbrellas, rubber, disperse, bullets, officers	**Riot (99th percentile)** violent, escalated, destructive, triggered, anti-government, and sparked.

Source: Authors

portrayal of the protesters as "fringe hooligans and mercenary criminals" (Fan, 2020)[22] further destabilized what had become a highly volatile situation.

As the "Hong Kong summer of uprising" (Lee et al., 2019: 1) unfolded, feelings of social danger prevailed in newspapers' accounts of events, with the use of the protest paradigm increasing in relevance. Citizens' willingness to assert their political and civic agency via marches and demonstrations was described more and more harshly over time. Articles pre-July 2019 focused on general descriptions of protesters' tactics, whereas post-June 2019 the writing prioritized detailed descriptions of violent actions that took place during the protests as well as mentions of the negative social impacts that such actions may cause, which are implied to be detrimental to the well-being of Hong Kong.

The spring and summer of 2019, however, was not the first time that the semantic context of protest keywords had become more polarizing and intense. As Table 4.4 shows, between 1998 and 2020 and particularly in 2014, the nature of neighboring terms for the word *riot* was similar to that found in the SCMP and the China Daily in the second half of June 2019. We speculate that the expansion and innovation of protests' tools and actions, and the inefficacy of the Hong Kong government's response to the protests may be the reasons why, in 2019, highly polarized protest keywords impacted the protests in such consequential way, whereas the impact of similar protest keywords was barely noticed in 2014, or between 1998 and 2020. This may signal constraint vis-à-vis diversity of opinions, which in turn points to diminishing freedom of speech.[23]

4.4.4 News Headline Analysis

News headlines are bait. They are meant to catch readers' attention by using narrative mechanisms and sensational or provoking words (Blom & Hansen, 2015) and help the reader get the most news with minimum effort (Dor, 2003). Headlines enjoy a privileged position that is explicitly reflected by a distinct layout and typography (White, 2011) – though the large-type, front page headline did not come into

[22] https://www.newyorker.com/news/daily-comment/telling-the-stories-of-the-protests-here-and-in-hong-kong

[23] https://www.hrw.org/node/379021

use until the late nineteenth century, when increased competition between newspapers led to the use of attention-getting headlines (Evans, 1974).

According to Scacco and Muddiman (2019) there are four types of news headlines based on their style. There are "restrained and traditional headlines" (2019: 433), which provide a short, clear and unambiguous overview of what can be read in the article. Creative language headlines can include humor or figurative language, and "sensational headlines" (2019: 447) are intended to help journalists make the story more interesting and unique by adding sensation. Finally, there are headlines that make readers curious "because of their special storytelling style" (2019: 430). Opposite to traditional headlines, certain information is withheld, or reference is made to particular information in the article, without revealing the clue in an effort to make readers curious and more likely to read the article.

Sometimes news headlines highlight a single element from the news article or a quote from someone mentioned in the article. Bell (1991) and Nir (1993) distinguish between headlines based on their function. According to Dor (2003), news headlines are *relevance optimizers*, designed to make the relevance of articles clear to the reader through *shortcuts* (Kronrod & Engel, 2001; Blake, 2007) that make the news headline vague enough to make the reader curious about it. Scacco and Muddiman (2015) identify four functions for news headlines. The first and most important function of a headline is "story summarization" (2015: 433) to provide the reader with a short and clear presentation of key information from the article. A second function is "interest generation" (2015: 430) to lure readers into the story and ensure that readers read the article. A third function of news headlines is immediacy satisfaction, intended to immediately satisfy the readers' need for what an article could be about. Readers who take the time to read their newspapers, or even just a few articles from beginning to end, are outnumbered by a growing number of readers who prefer to scan the news. So, it is important to create headlines that have a high information value in themselves, without readers having to necessarily to read the article. The fourth function of news headlines is attention direction (Stroud & Muddiman, 2015) which leads the reader to pay more attention to certain portions of the article. As no headline can combine the four functions together, the art of formulating a good and effective headline lies in the newspapers trying to incorporate as many of the four functions as possible. News headlines must be just enough convincing and seductive to drive readers to read the rest of the content associated to them (Ecker et al., 2014).

What are the function and style used in headlines vis-à-vis incidents of civic unrest in Hong Kong? Building on Luther and Zhou (2005), we answered this by testing our article corpus for the length and sentiment of headlines.

Sixty-three percent (63%) of articles in our dataset have long headlines (i.e., include six or more words), whereas the remaining 36% have headlines with less than six words, with these trends not varying significantly over the timeline of the research. With headlines like "The Worst of Times"[24] or "Hong Kong: A City

[24] The New York Times, October 12, 2019.

Divided",[25] the NYT emerges as the newspaper with the highest likelihood of having telegraphic headlines (i.e., 6.3 times more likely). With headlines like "Hong Kong Journalist Groups Rebuke Protesters for Harassing TV Cameraman at anti-extradition Rally",[26] "Hong Kong Extradition Bill: Business Groups Breathe Collective Sigh of Relief Over Government Decision to Delay Legislation",[27] or "Hong Kong Chief Executive Carrie lam Accuses Anti-Extradition Bill Protesters of 'Organizing a Riot'",[28] the SCMP emerges as the least likely of the newspapers to have short headlines (i.e., 11% less likely).[29] An in-depth analysis of the corpus headlines points to the NYT being the one newspaper that combines *restrained and traditional headlines* with *sensational headlines* to offer a clear and dramatic view of what the article is about it, which in turn stimulates its readership's curiosity. SCMP's long headlines showcase key information from the articles, and in consistently doing this, the SCMP emerges as the newspapers that more efficiently succeeds at both *story summarization*, *immediacy satisfaction*, and *attention direction* among all newspapers.

Headlines can be structurally classified as either verbal or nonverbal. Verbal headlines are those that contain a verbal clause, and according to Quirk et al. there are three main types of verbal clauses: "finite clause," "nonfinite clause," and "verbless clause" (1985: 992). Nonverbal headlines are those that contain a noun or a nominal phrase. Some 75% of the NYT headlines in our corpus were of the nonverbal kind, and 25% of the verbal type, with most of the nonverbal headlines being *modified* (1985: 65). Furthermore, on average, about 53% of the headlines of western-based newspapers other than the NYT were also of the nonverbal kind. This type of headlines is very effective in building a relationship with the reader, anticipating how they might feel about a particular topic, and influencing the readers' understanding of the article text.

We also found that, in their headlines, western-based newspapers used "presupposition" (van Dijk, 1995: 273) 45% more than Hong Kong-based newspapers. Through existential presupposition, writers presuppose a negative attribute for what articles identify as *others* (e.g., Hong Kong Chief Executive; Hong Kong government; Beijing; China; police; etc.) and positive ones for *us* (e.g., protesters; citizens; rights; freedoms; etc.). Through lexical presupposition, newspapers leveraged certain lexical items, or loaded words, for articles' headlines to deliver their intended message (Yule, 1996; Huckin, 2002). Moreover, headlines in Hong Kong- and western-based newspapers took advantage of metonymy, a figure of speech in which

[25] Ibid. November 24, 2019.

[26] The South China Morning Post, June 30, 2019.

[27] Ibid. June 17, 2019.

[28] Ibid. June 13, 2019.

[29] The full regression model containing all predictors was statistically significant, X^2 (8; (N = 4522) = 723.787, $p < 0.001$. The model correctly classified 75% of cases, and explained between 16.9% (Cox and Snell R^2) and 21.5% (Nagelkerke R^2) of the cases. The strongest predictor for short headlines is the variable for *The New York Times*, with an Exp(β) of 6.3, whereas the weakest predictor for short headlines is the variable for the *SCMP*, with an Exp(β) of – 0.89.

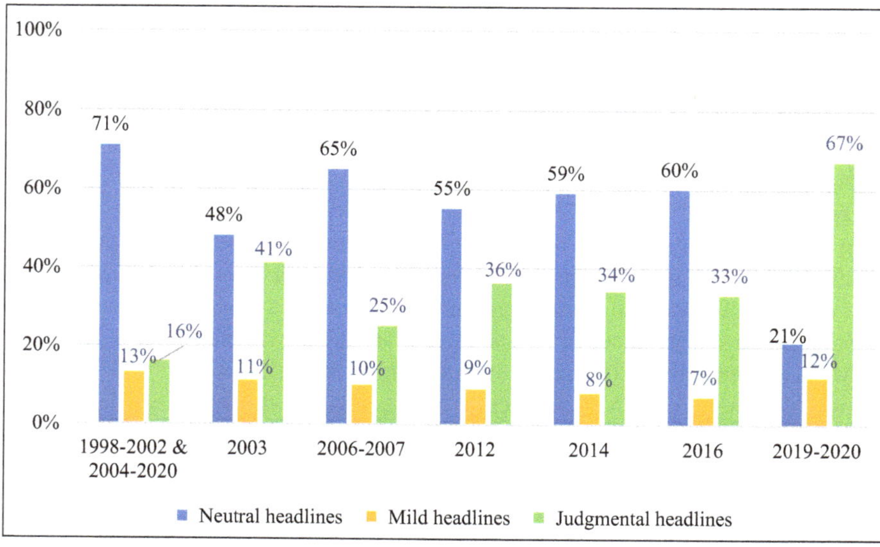

Fig. 4.9 Newspaper headline sentiment 1998–2020. (Source: Authors)

one word or phrase is substituted for another with which it is closely associated (e.g., names of countries to refer to either responsible institutions or social, economic, political status of countries). Data analysis revealed that the SCMP and the China Daily used metonymic reference in their headlines 35% more frequently than western-based newspapers, and especially in reference to democratic values, political and civil freedoms, and economic principles, which also supports Sbisà's argument about the suitability of presupposition "for transmitting a kind of contents which may be called ideological" (1999: 507).

Furthermore, we tested for the presence of judgmental words in headlines in the SCMP, the China Daily, and western-based newspapers to capture the extent to which headlines may have been critical or supportive of citizens' civic actions, and whether newspapers' support or criticism changed overtime. Statistical analysis revealed that, of all headlines, 54% are neutral, 36% judgmental, and 10% are mild. Moreover, as shown in Fig. 4.9, while the share of neutral headlines declines between 1998 and 2020 (going from 71% between 1998–2002 to 21% between 2019–2020), the share of judgmental headlines increases from 16% in 1998, to 67% in 2020. While neither the decrease in neutral headlines nor the increase in judgmental ones is linear, the fact that the share of mild headlines maintains a steadier trend overtime suggests that, from time to time and depending on the perception of the gravity of the episode of protests, neutral headlines may have been swapped for judgmental ones across both Hong Kong– and western-based newspapers. This is the case for headlines related to the anti–Article 23 protests of 2003 and anti–ELAB protests of 2019–2020.

Western-based newspapers are more likely to have judgmental headlines than the SCMP and the China Daily. With headlines like "Xi's Authoritarianism Clashes with West's Democratic Tradition"[30] or "Hong Kong Protests Cause Economic Clouds to Darken",[31] the *Financial Times* emerges as the newspaper being the most likely to have judgmental headlines (i.e., 3.5 times more likely), followed by the NYT (i.e., 2.9 more likely), the WSJ (i.e., 2.2 times more likely), and WaPo (i.e., 2 times more likely).[32] Sporting headlines like "City University Reveals Bill to Fix Vandalized Campus Will Run Hundreds of Millions of Dollars"[33] and "Why Is Beijing Quiet about the Opposition's Landslide District Election Victory?",[34] the SCMP and the China Daily are the least likely newspapers to have judgmental headlines (i.e., 52% less likely, and 80% less likely respectively). Moreover, the SCMP and the China Daily are more likely to have neutral headlines, with the China Daily being 4.2 times, and the SCMP being 2.4 times more likely to do so. Among western-based newspapers, the FT emerges as the least likely to have neutral headlines (i.e., 77% less likely), followed by the NYT (i.e., 65% less likely) and the WSJ (i.e., 53% less likely). WaPo is the exception as it is the only western-based newspapers likely to have neutral headlines (i.e., 1.9 times more likely).[35]

Between 1998 and 2020, both the SCMP, the China Daily and western-based newspapers used headlines as a perspective-inducing editorial tool, the compact representation of "a set of meanings, metaphors, representations, images, stories, and statements that produce a particular version of events" (Burr, 1995: 339). Newspapers chose emotive vocabulary and rhetorical devices to shape and foster readers' opinions on the relevance and impact of civic unrest for Hong Kong. In doing so, both the SCMP, the China Daily and western-based newspapers revealed the political and national representations they wanted to circulate within Hong Kong, and thus capture an audience considerably wider than simply those who actually read the news story.

---

[30] The Financial Times, June 6, 2019.

[31] Ibid. October 14, 2019.

[32] The full regression model containing all predictors was statistically significant, X^2 (8; N = 4522) = 190.459, $p < 0.001$. The model correctly classified 68.7% of cases, and explained between 6.2% (Cox and Snell R^2) and 9.1% (Nagelkerke R^2). The strongest predictor for judgmental headlines is the variable for the *Financial Times*, with an Exp(β) of 3.5, followed by the variable for the *NYT* with an Exp(β) of 2.9, the variable for the *WSJ* with an Exp(β) of 2.2, and the variable for the *Washington Post* with an Exp(β) of 2. The weakest predictor for a judgmental headline is the variable for the *SCMP*, with an Exp(β) of – 0.20.

[33] The South China Morning Post, December 1, 2019.

[34] Ibid. December 2, 2019.

[35] The full regression model containing all predictors was statistically significant, X^2 (8; N = 4522) = 174.592, $p < 0.005$. The model correctly classified 71.7% of cases, and explained between 5.1% (Cox and Snell R^2) and 10.2% (Nagelkerke R^2). The strongest predictor for neutral headlines is the variable for the *China Daily* with an Exp(β) of 4.2, followed by the variable for the *SCMP* with an Exp(β) of 2.4, the *Washington Post* with an Exp(β) of 1.9. The weakest predictor for a neutral headline is the variable for the *Financial Times* with an Exp(β) of – 0.77, followed by the NYT with an Exp(β) of – 0.65, the WSJ with an Exp(β) of – 0.53.

Chapter 5
Conclusions

Even under British rule, freedom of the press was elusive in Hong Kong. The British colonial administration-imposed laws similar to those used in other colonies to ensure that the press would not oppose its rule. Shen "counted as many as 30 laws in Hong Kong that could be used to curb the freedom of the press" (1972: 31). In practice, these laws were seldom enforced, mostly because the press in the immediate post-war decades did not focus on social and political affairs in Hong Kong. Press freedom meant freedom to criticize both the Communist regime in the PRC and the KMT regime in Taiwan, but not freedom to challenge the colonial government (Chan & Lee, 1991). The Hong Kong Journalists Association became publicly more outspoken, and Hong Kong's citizens became more active in asserting their rights only by the mid-1980s, more than a century after British rule. The major impetus for more democratic procedures came in reaction to the Chinese military crackdown on protestors in Tiananmen Square on June 4, 1989, when over 1 million people demonstrated and demanded more democratic institutions to protect themselves from similar crackdowns after the handover. As July 1, 1997 approached, the Hong Kong as well as the international press began voicing significant concern about the future of the free press in Hong Kong.

Chinese officials, perhaps in an effort to end speculation, surprised the world with information about what would happen to freedom of the press in Hong Kong under Chinese sovereignty in the final months before the handover. On May 31, 1996, the Director of China's Hong Kong and Macau Affairs Office addressed the issue of media rights in the post-1997 era, stating "there will certainly be freedom of [the] press after 1997 (...) They can criticize the government. They can object to our policies. They can say anything they like, but with regard to action, they have to be careful. Freedom of [the] press has to be regulated by laws, you see."[1] Director Lu Ping conceded that Hong Kong's laws regulating the media would change, and

[1] Kathy Chen et al., *China's Foreign Minister Issues Warnings,* Wall Street Journal, Oct. 16, 1996, at A17 (quoting Qian Qichen).

G. M. D. Dore et al., *A Free Press, If You Can Keep It*, SpringerBriefs in Political Science,
https://doi.org/10.1007/978-3-031-27584-5_5

as an example he cited press *advocacy* for Taiwan independence, which "will absolutely not be allowed, once Hong Kong reverts to Chinese sovereignty."[2] Five months later, on October 15, 1996, China's Foreign Minister Qian Qichen[3] offered an even more restrictive definition of Hong Kong press freedom by stating that after July 1, 1997, "the Hong Kong media can put forward criticism, but not rumors or lies. Nor can they put forward personal attacks on the Chinese leaders."[4] Deftly deploying *strategic ambiguity*, Chinese leaders assured the world that "there will be 'no change in Hong Kong freedom of the press' but, at the same time, emphasized the 'relative and limited nature' of such freedom" (Foster, 1998: 769).

These remarks sparked criticism in Hong Kong and abroad, with critics charging that China had broken its promise to maintain "western-style freedom of the press in post–1997 Hong Kong" (Foster, 1998: 765), a promise believed to be enshrined in the 1984 Joint Sino-British Declaration[5] and in the Hong Kong Basic Law.[6] Perhaps because the promise of press freedom in the Joint Declaration is, at best, vague and indeterminate, press freedom did not immediately decline in Hong Kong following its return to China. However, a complex dynamic of *strategic interactions* between Beijing and the local media began to change the realities of press freedom in Hong Kong. In fact, our computational analysis of newspapers' coverage of protests has revealed that Beijing's ability to influence Hong Kong-based newspapers by co-opting media owners (Lee, 2007), setting norms of journalistic political correctness (Lau & To, 2002), employing strategic ambiguity (Cheung, 2003), and inducing self-censorship (Lee, 2007a) has, over time, resulted in shifts in journalistic paradigms (Chan & Lee, 1984) and a subtle and progressive erosion of press freedom.

Through a *contextualized understanding of the volume and timing of articles published*, we found that between 1998 and 2020, the SCMP and the China Daily published more articles about protests in Hong Kong than western-based newspapers – 3728 vs. 794 – except for 2014 when this trend was reversed – 131 vs. 236. Their coverage is consistent and sustained over time, whereas that of western-based newspapers is punctuated by sharps peaks and dips, and declines over time, most significantly between 2015–2020. Such marked differences in the volume and timing of protests' coverage created an opportunity for the SCMP and the China Daily to set the agenda for how protests are framed and reported. Moreover, a *Granger causality investigation of news coverage on protests' size*, paired with a qualitative review of the content of articles published in the SCMP, China Daily, and western-based newspapers, revealed that the Hong Kong-based newspapers played a *facilitator*, rather than a *mobilizer*, role vis-à-vis the protests, as their sole interest in

[2] Hong Kong Will Not Have Full Press Freedom, Reuters World Service, May 31, 1996, (quoting Lu Ping).

[3] https://www.nytimes.com/2017/05/11/world/asia/qian-qichen-dead-china-foreign-minister.html

[4] "China's Foreign Minister Issues Warnings", The Wall Street Journal, October 16, 1996: A17.

[5] https://commonslibrary.parliament.uk/research-briefings/cbp-8616/

[6] See footnote no. 14.

covering the protests rested on their news value and worthiness and not the reasons behind them. Over time, these practices have resulted in a less critical press, especially towards Hong Kong's issues which are of relevance to Beijing.

The *diachronic consistency with which the SCMP and the China Daily frame their coverage of protests* reveals the use of *thematic framing*, which increases the effectiveness of the protest paradigm in voicing criticism towards the protests in the abstract, without necessarily delegitimizing the act of protesting itself, nor directly criticizing Hongkongers as protesters. The SCMP and the China Daily use the *Finance* frame to highlight the negative consequences that the protests may have on Hong Kong as an international financial hub, and China' financial gateway and firewall. The *Mainland* frame emphasizes how the protests undermine Beijing's efforts to uphold the principles of *one country, two systems,*[7] whereas the *Chief Executive* frame underlines the government's duty to ensure that the rule of law prevails in Hong Kong. Finally, the *Police Violence* frame stresses the police's ultimate duty to maintain order and safety in Hong Kong. Editorially, thematic framing makes it easier for newspapers to have people identify the issue at the heart of the protests as a society-wide phenomenon rather than citizens' discontent directed at specific actions of the Hong Kong Administration or Beijing's government.

Stylometric differences across news sources reveal a significant negative tone in the Hong Kong–based newspapers' coverage of the protests. The SCMP emerges as the newspaper with the most negative tone in its coverage of the protests. Moreover, the China Daily and SCMP use the terms *democracy* and *freedom* less frequently than western-based newspapers and, generally, as qualifiers rather than as nouns. These rhetorical choices may be attributable to the type of articles that the SCMP and the China Daily publish when covering the protests. They focus relentlessly on the details of the protests, an editorial choice that lends itself to using the terms democracy and freedom sparingly and as qualifiers. It also avoids discussing the values that the terms democracy and freedom embody vis-à-vis the right of citizens to protest across the large body of articles published.

Our investigation of *word embedding neighborhoods revealed that protest-related keywords are used differently between the SCMP, the China Daily and Western-based newspapers* as well as how the contexts of protest-related keywords differ across news sources over time. Our research confirmed semantic divergence in certain keywords between Hong Kong- and western-based newspapers vis-à-vis particular episodes of protests, with the most significant semantic divergence found in the lexical usage of the words *riot*, *protests*, *occupation*, and *confrontation*. We also found that the SCMP and the China Daily systematically relate the terms' nearest neighbors to adversarial or hostile behavior, and use nouns in their singular form, which signals the editorial intention to criticize the values embodied in those nouns while reporting about them as objects or actions.

We found *differences-in-differences in how Hong Kong–based newspapers report on protests over time*. In the case of the 2019–2020 anti-ELAB protests, the

[7] See footnote no. 6.

semantic context of the protest keywords in the SCMP and the China Daily became more polarizing, compared with that of western-based newspapers. June 2019 emerges as a pivotal moment, after which the meaning of several keywords shifts for at least the remainder of 2019. In the first half of 2019, in fact, neighbors for *riots* include terms like *actions*, *open*, *engage*, and *taken* which are not charged and, in the context of either a reporting or an opinion piece, descriptively inform readers. However, in the second half of 2019, the nature of the neighboring terms for *riots* changes to include more polarizing terms such as *violent*, *escalated*, *destructive*, *triggered*, *anti-government*, and *sparked*.

While the use of these rhetorical and non-rhetorical tactics made covering issues involving conflict between Mainland China and Hong Kong "less problematic" (Lee, 2007: 145) for Hong Kong print media, it eliminated neither the challenge of covering hot issues in ways acceptable to Beijing nor the risk of becoming hostage to pressure from powerful local public opinion (Ngok, 2007) as shown by the closing of The Apple Daily and Stand News, following investigations by the national security police in the fall of 2021,[8] and the voluntary precautionary shutdown of Citizen News at the end of 2021, accompanied by a press release stating that "the rapid changes in society in the past two years and the deterioration of the media environment have prevented us from achieving our ideals without worry."[9]

Moreover, the use of tactics such as strategic interaction and cultural co-orientation to help Beijing re-shape the contours of press freedom in Hong Kong has been paired, more and more, with *administrative strategic ambiguity*. The Hong Kong Police's decision to stop recognizing journalists not registered with the government, and only to recognize/ treat as media professionals those journalists either registered with the Hong Kong government's Information Services Department or working for "internationally-known media groups"[10] is one such example. The Hong Kong Police recognize that while they have always respected press freedom and journalists' right to report, they face increased challenges in enforcing the law, and they claim that the new requirement "would facilitate policing, allowing front-line personnel to identify media representatives more efficiently and swiftly"[11] to avoid a repetition of the tensions between police officers and the press which took place during the 2019–2020 anti-ELAB protests. The registration requirements have raised major concerns about the future of the press freedom in the city, as they allow a state institution to decide who can have access to newsworthy events and

[8] https://www.cnn.com/2022/01/02/media/hong-kong-citizen-news-shuts-down-intl/index.html
https://www.reuters.com/business/media-telecom/hong-kong-police-arrest-6-current-or-former-staff-online-media-outlet-2021-12-28/

[9] https://thehill.com/policy/international/587925-pro-democracy-news-site-closing-in-hong-kong-after-police-raid-at

[10] https://hongkongfp.com/2020/09/23/hong-kong-police-say-new-journalists-definition-will-aid-frontline-officers-only-brief-selected-media-on-change/

[11] Ibid.

information and operate as journalists, and force those who do not meet the requirements to self-censor what events they decide to cover.[12]

Another example is the indirect criminalization of newspapers having a facilitating or mobilizing function vis-à-vis collective actions expressive of freedom of speech as protests. In early 2022, Chief Executive Lam denied that her government was cracking down on the media by stating:

> *(...) law enforcement actions have nothing to do with the so-called suppression of press freedom or suppression of democracy. (...) Journalism is not sedition. But seditious acts and activities and inciting other people through public acts and activities could not be condoned under the guise of news reporting. It should be very clear what is reporting of news, and what is seditious acts or activities to undermine national security. You cannot say that the freedom of press is eroded due to the closing of two media outlets when 5.4 percent more local news outlets have been registered since Hong Kong's national security law was implemented, and 9.4 percent more overseas outlets have also registered.*[13]

In light of the requirement to be either registered with Hong Kong government's Information Services Department or working for "internationally-known media groups" to be able to practice journalism, it is difficult to discern whether the statistics quoted by Chief Executive Lam represent an actual increase in the number of journalists or news outlets operating in Hong Kong, or the fact that already practicing journalists registered to meet the new requirements to practice journalism. If this was the case, then those numbers are tangible proof of a shrinking press freedom.

Our NLP analysis has uncovered rhetorical and non-rhetorical tactics that provide empirical evidence of how the boundaries of press freedom have been changing and that contradict Chief Executive Lam's confident statement that "the media landscape in Hong Kong is as vibrant as ever, as the administration has been firmly committed to safeguarding the freedoms of the press and speech since the handover."[14] These changes are making it increasingly difficult for the press to balance being an effective watchdog with managing its relationship with a politically assertive China. Unlike when the British colonial administration controlled the Hong Kong press, nowadays the space for maneuvering is small, if even present at all (Dore, 2022).

---

[12] Pre-September 2021, press credentials were issued by the Hong Kong Journalists Association, which has 604 full members, all undergoing a strict self-regulatory vetting process.

[13] https://www.reuters.com/world/asia-pacific/hong-kong-leader-says-she-cannot-accept-claims-press-freedom-faces-extinction-2022-01-04/

[14] Ibid.

References

Aarøe, L., & Petersen, M. (2018). Cognitive biases and communication strength in social networks: The case of episodic frames. *British Journal of Political Science., 50*, 1–21. https://doi.org/10.1017/S0007123418000273
Achen, C. H., & Snidal, D. (1989). Rational deterrence theory and comparative case studies. *World Politics, 41*(2), 143–169.
Agnone, J. (2007). Amplifying public opinion: The policy impact of the U.S. environmental movement. *Social Forces, 85*(4), 1593–1620.
Altheide, D. L. (2018). *Creating fear: News and the construction of crisis*. Routledge.
Angelov, D. (2020). Top2Vec: Distributed representations of topics. Eprint 2008.09470.
Baden, C., & Lecheler, S. (2012). Fleeting, fading, or far-reaching? A knowledge-based model of the persistence of framing effects. *Communication Theory, 22*(4), 359–382.
Baden, C., Pipal, C., Schoonvelde, M., Mariken, A., & van der Velden, C. G. (2021). Three gaps in computational text analysis methods for social sciences: A research agenda. *Communication Methods and Measures, 16*, 1–18. https://doi.org/10.1080/19312458.2021.2015574
Bednarek, M., Caple, H., & Huan, C. (2021). Computer-based analysis of news values: A case study on National day. *Reporting, Journalism Studies, 22*, 6.
Bell, A. (1991). *The language of news media*. Blackwell.
Bender, E. M. (2009). Linguistically Naïve! Language Independent: Why NLP Needs Linguistic Typology. In *Proceedings of the EACL 2009 Workshop on the interaction between linguistics and computational linguistics: Virtuous, vicious or vacuous?* (pp. 26–32). Association for Computational Linguistics.
Berelson, B. (1952). *Content analysis in communication research*. Free Press.
Bergsma, S., Post, M., & Yarowsky, D. (2012). Stylometric analysis of scientific articles. *HLT-NAACL*, 327–337.
Bhatia, A. (2015). Construction of discursive illusions in the 'Umbrella Movement'. *Discourse & Society, 26*(4), 407–427.
Blake, A. C. (2007). Media-generated shortcuts: Do newspaper headlines present another roadblock for low-information rationality? *The Harvard International Journal of Press/Politics, 12*, 24–43.
Blei, D. M., Ng, A. Y., & Jordan, M. I. (2003). Latent dirichlet allocation. *Journal of Machine Learning Research, 3*, 993–1022.
Blei, D. M., & Lafferty, J. D. (2007). A correlated topic model of science. *The Annals of Applied Statistics, 1*(1), 17–35.
Blom, J. N., & Hansen, K. R. (2015). Click bait: Forward-reference as lure in online news headlines. *Journal of Pragmatics, 76*, 87–100.

G. M. D. Dore et al., *A Free Press, If You Can Keep It*, SpringerBriefs in Political Science, https://doi.org/10.1007/978-3-031-27584-5

Blum, A., & Mitchell, T. (1998). Combining labeled and unlabeled data with co-training. In *Proceedings of the eleventh annual conference on computational learning theory, COLT '98* (pp. 92–100). Association for Computing Machinery.

Bouma, G. (2009). Normalized (pointwise) mutual information in collocation extraction. In *Proceedings of the biennial GSCL conference 2009*.

Boydstun, A. E., Gross, J. H., Resnik, P., & Smith, N. A. (2013). Identifying media frames and frame dynamics within and across policy issues. In *New directions in analyzing text as data workshop*, London.

Boykoff, J. (2006). Framing dissent: Mass-media coverage of the global justice movement. *New Political Science, 28*(2), 201–228.

Boyle, M. P., McLeod, D. M., & Armstrong, C. L. (2012). Adherence to the protest paradigm: The influence of protest goals and tactics on news coverage in U.S. and international newspapers. *International Journal of Press/Politics, 17*(2), 127–144.

Burr, V. (1995). *An introduction to social constructionism*. Routledge.

Büyüköz, B., Hürriyetoğlu, A., & Özgür, A. (2020). Analyzing ELMo and DistilBERT on socio-political news classification. In *Proceedings of the workshop on automated extraction of socio-political events from news* (pp. 9–18). European Language Resources Association (ELRA).

Chan, J. M., & Lee, C. C. (1984). Journalistic paradigms on civil protests: A case study of Hong Kong. In A. Arno & W. Dissanayake (Eds.), *The News Media in National and International Conflict* (pp. 183–202). Westview Press.

Chan, C. K. (2015). Contested news values and media performance during the umbrella movement. *Chinese Journal of Communication, 8*(4), 420–428.

Chan, J. M., & Chin, C. L. (1989). Shifting journalistic paradigms: Editorial stance and political transition in Hong Kong. *The China Quarterly, 117*(Mar), 97–117.

Chan, J. M., & Chin, Lee, C.-c. (1991). *Mass media and political transition: The Hong Kong Press in China's Orbit*. Guilford Press.

Chan, J. M., & Lee, F. L. (2007). Hong Kong. Ten years later media and politics in Hong Kong: A decade after the handover. *China Perspectives*, 2007/2.

Cheng, J. Y. (2014). The emergence of radical politics in Hong Kong: Causes and impact. *The China Review, 14*(1), 199–232.

Cheng, E. W. (2016). Street politics in a hybrid regime: The diffusion of political activism in post-colonial Hong Kong. *The China Quarterly, June*, 383–406.

Cheung, A. S. Y. (2003). Hong Kong press coverage of China-Taiwan cross-straits tension. In R. Ash, P. Ferdinand, H. Brian, R. Porter, & F. Ash (Eds.), *Hong Kong in transition* (pp. 210–225). Routledge.

Chong, D., & Druckman, J. (2007). Framing theory. *Annual Review of Political Science, 10*, 103–126. https://doi.org/10.1146/annurev.polisci

Cotter, C. (2010). *News talk: Investigating the language of journalism*. Cambridge University Press.

Dardis, F. E. (2006). Marginalization devices in U.S. Press coverage of Iraq war protest: A content analysis. *Mass Communication and Society, 9*(2), 117–135.

de Vreese, C. H. (2012). New avenues for framing research. *American Behavioral Scientist, 56*(3), 365–375.

Dehler-Holland, J., Schumacher, K., & Fichtner, W. (2021). Topic modeling uncovers shifts in media framing of the German renewable energy act. *Patterns (N Y), 2*(1), 100169.

Demszky, D., Garg, N., Voigt R., Zou, J., Gentzkow, M., Shapiro, J., & Jurafsky, D. (2019). Analyzing polarization in social media: Method and application to tweets on 21 mass shootings.

Devlin, J., Chang, M.-W., Lee, K., & Toutanova, K. (2019). BERT: Pre-training of Deep Bidirectional Transformers for Language Understanding. In *Proceedings of the 2019 conference of the North American chapter of the Association for Computational Linguistics: Human language technologies, Volume 1 (Long and short papers)* (pp. 4171–4186). Association for Computational Linguistics.

Dor, D. (2003). On newspaper headlines as relevance optimizers. *Journal of Pragmatics, 35*(5), 695–721.

Dore, G. M. D. (2022). Business as usual? The role of business elites in Hong Kong's evolving political identity. Special issue Chinese diasporas and transnational public spheres in the long 20th century. In H.-Y. Kuo & S. Van Morgan (Eds.), *Translocal Chinese: East Asian perspectives*. Forthcoming spring 2022.

Du, Y., Zhu, L., & Yang, F. (2018). A movement of varying faces: How "occupy central" was framed in the news in Hong Kong, Taiwan, mainland China, the UK, and the U.S. *International Journal of Communication, 12*, 2556.

Earl, J. M., McCarthy, J. D., & Soule, S. A. (2004). The use of newspaper data in the study of collective action. *Annual Review of Sociology, 30*(1), 65–80.

Ecker, U. K. H., Lewandowsky, S., Chang, E. P., & Pillai, R. (2014). The effects of subtle misinformation in news headlines. *Journal of Experimental Psychology: Applied, 20*(4), 323–335.

Eilders, C. (2006). News factors and news decisions. Theoretical and methodological advances in Germany. *Communications, 31*(1), 5–24.

Entman, R. (1993). Framing: Toward clarification of a fractured paradigm. *Journal of Communication, 43*(4), 51–58.

Evans, H. (1974). *News headlines (Editing and design)*. Holt, Rinehart and Winston.

Fan, J. (2020). Telling the stories of the protests here and in Hong Kong. The New Yorker, June 23.

Fernandes, J. (2013). Effects of negative political advertising and message repetition on candidate evaluation. *Mass Communication and Society, 16*, 268–291.

Field, A., Kliger, D., Wintner, S., Pan, J., Jurafsky, D., & Tsvetkov, Y. (2018). Framing and agenda-setting in Russian news: A computational analysis of intricate political strategies. In *Proceedings of the 2018 Conference on empirical methods in natural language processing* (pp. 3570–3580). Association for Computational Linguistics.

Foster, F. S. (1998). The illusory promise: Freedom of the Press in Hong Kong, China. *Indiana Law Journal, 73*(3), 765–793.

Freeman, J. R. (1983). Granger causality and the times series analysis of political relationships. *American Journal of Political Science, 27*(2), 327–358.

Fulcher, G. (2010). *Practical language testing* (1st ed.). Routledge.

Fung, A. Y. H., & Lee, C. C. (1994). Hong Kong's changing media ownership: Uncertainty and dilemma. *Gazette (Leiden, Netherlands), 53*(1–2), 127–133.

Galtung, J., & Ruge, M. H. (1965). The structure if foreign news: The presentation of the Congo, Cuba, and Cyprus in four Norwegian newspapers. *Journal of Peace Research, 2*(1), 65–91.

Gamson, W. A., & Wolfsfeld, G. (1993). Movements and media as interacting systems. *Annals of the American Academy of Political and Social Science, 528*, 114–125.

Gans, H. (2004). *Democracy and the news*. Oxford University Press.

Glasser, T. L. (1992). Objectivity precludes responsibility. In E. D. Cohen (Ed.), *Philosophical issues in journalism* (pp. 166–175). Oxford University Press.

Gonen, H., Jawahar, G., Seddah, D., & Goldberg, Y. (2020). Simple, interpretable and stable method for detecting words with usage change across corpora. In *Proceedings of the 58th annual meeting of the Association for Computational Linguistics* (pp. 538–555). Online. Association for Computational Linguistics.

Granger, C. W. J. (1980). Testing for causality: A personal viewpoint. *Journal of Economic Dynamics and Control, 2*, 329–352; and Clive W. J. Granger. *Essays in econometrics: The collected papers of Clive W.J. Granger*. Cambridge University Press.

Gross, K. (2008). Framing persuasive appeals: Episodic and thematic framing, emotional response, and policy opinion. *Political Psychology, 29*, 169–192.

Hackett, R. A., & Zhao, Y. (1994). Challenging a master narrative: Peace protest and opinion/editorial discourse in the US press during the Gulf War. *Discourse & Society, 5*(4), 509–541.

Hallin, D., & Mancini, P. (2004). *Comparing media systems: Three models of media and politics*. Cambridge University Press.

Hamilton, W. L., Leskovec, J., & Jurafsky, D. (2016). Diachronic word embeddings reveal statistical laws of semantic change. In *Proceedings of the 54th annual meeting of the Association for*

Computational Linguistics (Volume 1: Long papers) (pp. 1489–1501). Germany. Association for Computational Linguistics.

Harcup, T., & O'Neill, D. (2017). What is news? News values revisited (again). *Journalism Studies, 18*(12), 1470–1488.

HKSAR Government. (2007). Note for Public Works Subcommittee of Finance Committee: Supplementary Information on 728CL—Preservation of Queen's Pier. http://www.legco.gov.hk/yr06-07/english/fc/pwsc/papers/pi07-03e.pdf

Hofmann, V., Pierrehumbert, J. B., & Hinrich Schutze, H. (2021). Dynamic contextualized word embeddings. Eprint 2010.12684.

Holm, S. (1979). A simple sequentially rejective multiple test procedure. *Scandinavian Journal of Statistics, 6*, 65–70.

Huckin, T. (2002). Critical discourse analysis and the discourse of condescension. In E. Barton & G. Stygall (Eds.), *Discourse studies in composition*. Hampton Press.

Hürriyetoğlu, A., Yörük, E., Yüret, D., Yoltar, G. C. B., Durus, F., Mutlu, O., & Akdemir, A. (2019). Overview of CLEF 2019 lab protest news: Extracting protests from news in a cross-context setting. In *International conference of the cross-language evaluation forum for European languages* (pp. 425–432). Springer.

Hutcheon, T. (1998). *Pressing concerns: Hong Kong's Media in an era of transition.* Discussion paper D-32. The Joan Shorenstein Center on the Press, Politics and Public Policy, John F. Kennedy School of Government. Harvard University Press.

Ibrahim, Z., & Lam, J. (Eds.). (2020). *Rebel City: Hong Kong's year of water and fire*. South China Morning Post and World Scientific.

Jacobi, C., van Atteveldt, W., & Welbers, K. (2016). Quantitative analysis of large amounts of journalistic texts using topic modelling. *Digital Journalism, 4*(1), 89–106.

Jatowt, A., & Duh, K. (2014). A framework for analyzing semantic change of words across time. In *IEEE/ACM joint conference on digital libraries* (pp. 229–238). https://doi.org/10.1109/JCDL.2014.6970173

Kennedy, K. J., & Kuang, X. (2014). National identity and patriotism in Hong Kong's education reform: Student attributes and contested curriculum structures. In C. Marsh & J. C. K. Lee (Eds.), *Asia's high performing education systems: The case of Hong Kong*. Routledge.

Kenyon-Dean, K., Fujimoto, A. E., Georges-Filteau, J., Glasz, C., Kaur, B., Lalande, A., Bhanderi, S., Belfer, R., Kanagasabai, N., Sarrazingendron, R., Verma, R., & Ruths, D. (2018). Sentiment analysis: It's complicated! In *Proceedings of the 2018 conference of the North American chapter of the Association for Computational Linguistics: Human language technologies, Volume 1 (Long papers)* (pp. 1886–1895). Association for Computational Linguistics.

King, B. G. (2011). The tactical disruptiveness of social movements: Sources of market and mediated disruption in corporate boycotts. *Social Problems, 58*(4), 491–517.

Koon, L., Wong, H. H., Chi-Kin Lee, J., Kerry, J. K., & Chan, J. K.-s. (2021). A proposed model for teachers' perceptions of national and moral education: A national identity building curriculum in post-colonial Hong Kong. *Journal of Educational Change, 22*, 221–246.

Koppel, M., Schler, J., & Zigdon, K. (2005). Determining an author's native language by mining a text for errors. In *Proceedings of the eleventh ACM SIGKDD international conference on knowledge discovery in data mining, KDD '05* (pp. 624–628). Association for Computing Machinery.

Kronrod, A., & Engel, O. (2001). Accessibility theory and referring expressions in newspaper headlines. *Journal of Pragmatics, 33*(5), 683–699.

Kuah-Pearce, K. E., & Guiheux, G. (Eds.). (2009). *Social movements in China and Hong Kong: The expansion of protest space*. Amsterdam University Press.

Kuiken, J., Schuth, A., Spitters, M., & Marx, M. (2017). Effective headlines of newspaper articles in a digital environment. *Digital Journalism, 5*(10), 1300–1314.

Kulkarni, V., Al-Rfou, R., Perozzi, B., & Skiena, S. (2015). Statistically significant detection of linguistic change. In *Proceedings of the 24th international conference on World Wide Web,*

WWW '15 (pp. 625–635). Republic and Canton of Geneva, CHE. International World Wide Web Conferences Steering Committee.

Kwong, Y. (2015). The dynamics of mainstream and internet alternative Media in Hong Kong: A case study of the umbrella movement. *International Journal of China Studies, 6*(3), 273–295.

Lau, T., & To, Y.-m. (2002). Walking a tight rope: Hong Kong's media facing political and economic challenges since sovereignty transfer. In K. C. Ming & Y. A. So (Eds.), *Crisis and transformation in China's Hong Kong*. Routledge.

Lau, J. H., Newman, D., & Baldwin, T. (2014). Machine reading tea leaves: Automatically evaluating topic coherence and topic model quality. In *Proceedings of the 14th conference of the European chapter of the Association for Computational Linguistics* (pp. 530–539).

Lawrence, S. V., & Martin, M. F. (2020). China's National Security Law for Hong Kong: Issues for congress. Congressional Research Service. https://crsreports.congress.gov. R46473.

Le, E. (2012). Gateways to the news: Headlines on Le Monde's home page and front page. *Discourse, Context & Media, 1*(1), 32–44.

Lee, C.-C. (1998). Press self-censorship and political transition in Hong Kong. *Harvard International Journal of Press/Politics., 3*(2), 55–73.

Lee, F. L. F. (2006). Collective efficacy, support for democratization, and political participation in Hong Kong. *International Journal of Public Opinion Research., 18*(3), 297–317.

Lee, F. L. F. (2007a). Strategic interaction, cultural co-orientation, and press freedom in Hong Kong. *Asian Journal of Communication, 17*(2), 134–147.

Lee, F. L. F. (2007b). Objectivity as self-censorship? Hong Kong citizens' beliefs in media neutrality and perceptions of press freedom. *Asian Survey, 47*(3), 434–454.

Lee, F. L. F. (2014). Triggering the protest paradigm: Examining factors affecting news coverage of protests. *International Journal of Communication, 8*.

Lee, F. L. F. (2018). Changing political economy of the Hong Kong media. *China Perspectives* [Online], 2018/3 | 2018, Online since 1 Sept 2018.

Lee, F. L. F., & Chan, J. M. (2008). Making sense of participation: The political culture of pro-democracy demonstrators in Hong Kong. *The China Quarterly, 193*, 84–101.

Lee, F. L. F., & Chan, J. (2009). Organizational production of self-censorship in the Hong Kong media. *The International Journal of Press/Politics, 14*(1), 112–133.

Lee, F. L. F., & Chan, J. M. (2013). Exploring Hong Kong as the "movement society": An analysis of the form and development of contentious collective action of Hong Kong. In S. K. Cheung, K. C. Leung, & K. M. Chan (Eds.), *Hong Kong, discourse, media* (pp. 243–269). Oxford University Press.

Lee, P. S. N., & Chu, L. (1998). Inherent dependence on power: The Hong Kong Press in Political Transition. *Media, Culture & Society, 20*(1), 59–77.

Lee, F. L. F., & Lin, A. M. Y. (2006). Newspaper editorial discourse and the politics of self-censorship in Hong Kong. *Discourse & Society, 7*(3), 331–358.

Lee, F. L. F., Yuen, S., Tang, G., & Cheng, E. W. (2019). Hong Kong's summer of uprising: From anti-extradition to anti-authoritarian protests. *The China Review, 19*(4), 1–32.

Li, J. (2019). Hong Kong-China extradition plans explained. *BBC News*.

Liebes, T., & Blum-Kulka, S. (2004). It takes two to blow the whistle: Do journalists control the outbreak of scandal? *American Behavioral Scientist, 47*(9), 1153–1170.

Lorenz, A. L., & Vivian, J. (1996). *News: Reporting and writing*. Allyn and Bacon.

Lucy, L., Demszky, D., Bromley, P., & Jurafsky, D. (2020). Content analysis of textbooks via natural language processing: Findings on gender, race, and ethnicity in Texas U.S. history textbooks. *AERA Open, 6*(3), 2332858420940312.

Luther, C. A., & Zhou, X. (2005). Within the boundaries of politics: News framing of SARS in China and the United States. *Journalism and Mass Communication Quarterly, 82*(4), 857–872.

Ma, N. (2007). State-press relationship in post-1997 Hong Kong; constant negotiation amidst self-restraint. *The China Quarterly, 192*, 949–970.

Ma, N. (2011). Value changes and legitimacy crisis in post-industrial Hong Kong. *Asian Survey, 51*(4), 683–712.

Martin, M. (2019). Hong Kong's proposed extradition law amendments. *Congressional Research Service*. loc.gov, 7-2199.

Matthes, J., & Kohring, M. (2008). The content analysis of media frames: Toward improving reliability and validity. *Journal of Communication, 58*(2), 258–279.

McCallum, A. K. (2002). Mallet: A machine learning for language toolkit. http://mallet.cs.umass.edu

McCann, B., Bradbury, J., Xiong, C., & Socher, R. (2017). Learned in translation: Contextualized Word Vectors. *Advances in Neural Information Processing Systems, 30*.

McCarthy, A. D., Yancey, K. P., LaFlair, G. T., Egbert, J., Liao, M., & Settles, B. (2021, November). Jump-starting item parameters for adaptive language tests. In *Proceedings of the 2021 conference on empirical methods in natural language processing* (pp. 883–899).

McCluskey, M., Stein, S., Boyle, M., & Mcleod, D. (2009). Community structure and social protest: Influences on newspaper coverage. *Mass Communication and Society, 12*, 353–371.

McCombs, M., & Ghanem, S. I. (2001). The convergence of agenda setting and framing. In S. D. Reese, O. H. Gandy, & A. Grant (Eds.), *Framing public life: Perspectives on media and our understanding of the social world* (pp. 67–81). Laurence Erlbaum Associates Publishers.

McFarlane, T., & Hay, I. (2003). The battle for Seattle: Protest and popular geopolitics in the Australian newspaper. *Political Geography, 22*, 211–232. https://doi.org/10.1016/S0962-6298(02)00090-2

McInnes, L., & Healy, J. (2017). Accelerated hierarchical density based clustering. *IEEE International Conference on Data Mining Workshops (ICDMW), 2017*, 33–42.

McInnes, L., et al. (2018). UMAP: Uniform manifold approximation and projection. *Journal of Open Source Software, 3*(29), 861. https://doi.org/10.21105/joss.00861

McLeod, D. M., & Hertog, J. K. (1998). Social control and the mass media's role in the regulation of protest groups: The communicative acts perspective. In D. Demers & K. Viswanath (Eds.), *Mass media, social control and social change* (pp. 305–330). Iowa State University Press.

McLeod, D. M., & Detenber, B. H. (1999). Framing effects of television news coverage of social protest. *Journal of Communication, 49*(3), 3–23.

McLeod, D. M., & Hertog, J. K. (1999). Social control and the mass media's role in the regulation of protest groups: The Communicative Acts perspective. In D. Demers & K. Viswanath (Eds.), *Mass media, social control and social change* (pp. 305–330). Iowa State University Press.

McQuail, D., & Windahl, S. (1993). *Communication models for the study of mass communications*. Routledge.

Mihalcea, R. (2012). Multilingual natural language processing. In *Proceedings of the workshop on innovative hybrid approaches to the processing of textual data* (p. 45). Association for Computational Linguistics.

Miller, G. A. (1995). WordNet: A lexical database for English. *Communication. ACM, 38*(11), 39–41.

Mimno, D., Wallach, H., Talley, E., Leenders, M., & McCallum, A. (2011). Optimizing semantic coherence in topic models. In *Proceedings of the 2011 conference on empirical methods in natural language processing* (pp. 262–272). Association for Computational Linguistics.

Mohammad, S. (2018). Obtaining reliable human ratings of valence, arousal, and dominance for 20,000 English words. In *Proceedings of the 56th annual meeting of the association for computational linguistics (Volume 1: Long papers)* (pp. 174–184). Association for Computational Linguistics.

Mosteller, F., & Wallace, D. L. (1984). *Applied Bayesian and classical inference: The case of the federalist papers*. Springer.

Ng, M. K. (2020). The making of 'violent' Hong Kong: A centennial dream? A fight for democracy? A challenge to humanity? *Planning Theory & Practice, 21*(3), 483–494.

Ngok, K. (2007). Chinese education policy in the context of decentralization and marketization: Evolution and implications. *Asia Pacific Education Review, 8*(1), 142–157.

Nir, R. (1993). A discourse analysis of news headlines. *Hebrew Linguistics, 37*, 23–31.

Oliver, M. B., Raney, A., & Bryant, J. (2019). *Media effects: Advances in theory and research.* Routledge.
Ott, M., Cardie, C., & Hancock, J. T. (2013). Negative deceptive opinion spam. In *Proceedings of the 2013 conference of the North American chapter of the Association for Computational Linguistics: Human language technologies* (pp. 497–501). Association for Computational Linguistics.
Overholt, W. (2019). *Hong Kong: The rise and fall of "One Country, Two Systems"*. Harvard Kennedy School.
Pennebaker, J. W., Boyd, R. L., Jordan, K., & Blackburn, K. (2015). The development and psychometric properties of LIWC. Technical report.
Peters, M. E., Neumann, M., Iyyer, M., Gardner, M., Clark, C., Lee, K., & Zettlemoyer, L. (2018). Deep contextualized word representations. *NAACL 2018.*
Price, V., Tewksbury, D., & Powers, E. (1997). Switching trains of thought: The impact of news frames on readers' cognitive responses. *Communication Research, 24*(5), 481–506.
Purbrick, M. (2019). A report pf the 2019 Hong Kong protests. *Asian Affairs, 50*(4), 465–487.
Quirk, R., Greenbaum, S., Leech, G., & Svatvik, J. (1985). *A comprehensive grammar of the English Language*. Longman.
Ramzy, A. & Yu, E. (2019). Hong Kong's leader, Carrie Lam, to withdraw extradition bill that ignited protests. *The New York Times.*
Reimers, N., & Gurevych, I. (2019, November). Sentence-BERT: Sentence embeddings using Siamese BERT-networks. In *Proceedings of the 2019 conference on empirical methods in natural language processing and the 9th international joint conference on natural language processing (EMNLP-IJCNLP)* (pp. 3982–3992).
Rudolph, M., & Blei, D. (2018). Dynamic embeddings for language evolution. In *WWW 2018: The 2018 Web conference*, April 23–27, 2018. ACM.
Salton, G., Wong, G. A., & Yang, C. S. (1975). A vector space model for automatic indexing. *Communications of the ACM, 18*(11), 613–620.
Sandeep Soni, S., Klein, L. F., & Eisenstein, J. (2021). Abolitionist networks: Modeling language change in nineteenth-century activist newspapers. *Journal of Cultural Analytics, 6*(1), 1–43.
Sanh, V., Debut, L., Chaumond, J., & Wolf, T. (2019). DistilBERT, a distilled version of BERT: Smaller, faster, cheaper and lighter. *CoRR*, abs/1910.01108.
Sbisà, M. (1999). Ideology and persuasive presuppositions. In J. Verschueren (Ed.), *Language and ideology: Selected papers from the 6th international pragmatic conference* (Vol. 1, pp. 492–509). International Pragmatic Association.
Scacco, J. M., & Muddiman, A. (2019). The curiosity effect: Information seeking in the contemporary news environment. *New Media & Society, 22*(3), 429–448.
Schrodt, P. A., Simpson, E. M., & Gerner, D. J. (2001). Monitoring conflict using automated coding of newswire reports: A comparison of five geographical regions. In *Conference 'Identifying Wars: Systematic conflict research and it's utility in conflict resolution and prevention'* (pp. 8–9). Citeseer.
Schulz, A., Wettstein, M., & Wirth, W. (2014, May). All hostile media: Group membership, ingroup identification and consonance of news reporting as moderator of the hostile media effect. Paper presented at the annual meeting of the international communication association (ICA).
Shen, J. C. Y. (1972). *The law and mass media in Hong Kong*. Mass Communications Center, The Chinese University of Hong Kong.
Shen, F. (2004). Chronic accessibility and individual cognitions: Examining the effects of message frames in political advertisements. *Journal of Communication, 54*(1), 123–137.
Shirk, S. (Ed.). (2011). *Changing media, changing China*. Oxford University Press.
Shoemaker, P. J., & Reese, S. D. (1996). *Mediating the message: Theories of influences on mass media content*. Longman Publishers.
Sia, S., Dalmia A., & Mielke, S. J. (2020). Tired of topic models? Clusters of pretrained word embeddings make for fast and good topics too! In *Proceedings of the 2020 conference on empirical methods in natural language processing*.

Sinclair, K., & Ng, N. K.-c. (1997). *Asia's finest marches on: Policing Hong Kong from 1841 into the 21st century*. Kevin Sinclair Associates Ltd.
Snow, D., & Benford, R. D. (1988). Ideology, frame resonance, and participant mobilization. In B. Klandermans, H. Kriesi, & S. Tarrow (Eds.), *From structure to action* (pp. 197–217). JAI Press.
Snyder, D., & Kelly, W. R. (1977). Conflict intensity, media sensitivity and the validity of newspaper data. *American Sociological Review, 42*(1), 105–123.
So, A. Y. (2011). The transformation of social movements in Hong Kong after 1997. In J. Broadbent & V. Brockman (Eds.), *East Asian social movements: Power, protest and change* (pp. 365–384). Springer.
So, A. Y., & Ping, L.-I. (2020). Civic localism, anti-mainland localism, and independence: The changing pattern of identity politics in Hong Kong special administrative region. *Asian Education and Development Studies, 9*(2), 255–267.
Socher, R., Perelygin, A., Wu, J., Chuang, J., Manning, C. D., Ng, A., & Potts, C. (2013). Recursive deep models for semantic compositionality over a sentiment tree-bank. In *Proceedings of the 2013 Conference on empirical methods in natural language processing* (pp. 1631–1642). Association for Computational Linguistics.
Sparks, C. (2015). Business as usual: The UK national daily press and the occupy central movement. *Chinese Journal of Communication, 8*(4), 429–446.
Stephens, K. K., & Rains, S. A. (2011). Information and communication technology sequences and message repetition in interpersonal interaction. *Communication Research, 38*(1), 101–122.
Strange, J. J., & Leung, C. C. (1999). How anecdotal accounts in news and fiction can influence judgments of a social problem's urgency, causes, and cures. *Personality and Social Psychology Bulletin, 25*(4), 436–449.
Stroud, N. J., Muddiman, A., & Scacco, J. M. (2015). *Engaging audiences via online news sites* (p. 922). Communication Faculty Publications.
Tausczik, Y. R., & Pennebaker, J. W. (2010). The psychological meaning of words: Liwc and computerized text analysis methods. *Journal of Language and Social Psychology, 29*(1), 24–54.
Tenney, I., Dipanjan, D., & Pavlick, E. (2019). BERT rediscovers the classical NLP pipeline. In *Proceedings of the 57th annual meeting of the Association for Computational Linguistics (2019)* (pp. 4593–4601).
The Government of China. *National committee of the Chinese People's political consultative conference*. Accessed on October 12, 2012. http://en.cppcc.gov.cn
The Government of China. *China's National people congress*. Accessed on October 12, 2021. http://www.npc.gov.cn/englishnpc/
Ting, C.-C. (2013). The star and the queen: Heritage conservation and the emergence of a new Hong Kong subject. *Modern Chinese Literature and Culture, 25*(2), 80–129.
Trilling, D., Tolochko, P., & Burscher, B. (2017). From newsworthiness to shareworthiness: How to predict news sharing based on article characteristics. *Journalism & Mass Communication Quarterly, 94*(1), 38–60.
Trilling, D., van Atteveldt, W., & Arcila Calderon, C. (2022). *Computational analysis of communication*. Wiley.
Tse, K. C. T. (2013). 國民身份教育可以怎麼辦?[How could teach national identity?]. Paper presented at invited seminar on citizenship education: Challenges of nationalism and globalization, June 20–21, 2013, the Hong Kong Institute of Education.
Tsfati, Y. & Walter, N. (2019). The world of news and politics. *Media Effects: Advances in Theory and Research.*
Tsui, H. (2007). The demolition of Star Ferry Pier: Urban reclamation versus cultural heritage in Hong Kong. Eurozin (Oct. 29). http://www.eurozine.com/articles/2007-10-29-tsui-en.html
Tuchman, G., & Tuchman, B. W. (1978). *Making news: A study in the construction of reality*. Free Press.

Tuukka, Y.-A., Eranti, V., & Kukkonen, A. (2022). Topic modeling for frame analysis: A study of media debates on climate change in India and USA. *Global Media and Communication, 18*(1), 91–112.
Valkenburg, P. M., Semetko, H. A., & De Vreese, C. H. (1999). The effects of news frames on readers' thoughts and recall. *Communication Research, 26*, 550–569.
van der Pas, D. J., van der Brug, W., & Rens, V. (2017). Political parallelism in media and political agenda-setting. *Political Communication, 34*(4), 491–510.
van Dijk, T. A. (1995). Discourse semantics and ideology. *Discourse and Society, 6*, 243–289.
van Gorp, B. (2005). Where is the frame? Victims and intruders in the Belgian press coverage of the asylum issue. *European Journal of Communication, 20*(4), 484–507.
Verba, S. (1996). The citizen as respondent: Sample surveys and American democracy. *American Political Science Review, 90*(1), 1–7.
Verba, S., Schlozman, K. L., Brady, H., & Nie, N. H. (1993). Citizen activity: Who participates? What do they say? *The American Political Science Review, 87*(2), 303–318.
Verba, S., Schlozman, K. L., & Brady, H. E. (1995). *Voice and equality: Civic voluntarism in American politics*. Harvard University Press.
Victor, D, & May, T. (2019). The murder case that lit the fuse in Hong Kong. *The New York Times*.
Weaver, D. A., & Scacco, J. M. (2013). Revisiting the protest paradigm: The tea party as filtered through prime-time cable news. *International Journal of Press/Politics, 18*(1), 61–84.
Welbers, K., van Atteveldt, W., Kleinnijenhuis, J., Ruigrok, N., & Schaper, J. (2016). News selection criteria in the digital age: Professional norms versus online audience metrics. *Journalism, 17*, 1–17.
Wendlandt, L., Kummerfeld, J. K., & Mihalcea, R. (2018). Factors influencing the surprising instability of word embeddings. In *Proceedings of the 2018 Conference of the North American chapter of the Association for Computational Linguistics: Human language technologies, Volume 1 (Long papers)* (pp. 2092–2102). Association for Computational Linguistics.
Wijaya, D. T., & Yeniterzi, R. (2011). Understanding semantic change of words over centuries. In *Proceedings of the 2011 international workshop on DETecting and Exploiting Cultural diversiTy on the social web (DETECT '11)* (pp. 35–40). Association for Computing Machinery.Wong, H. T., & Liu, S.-D. (2018). Cultural activism during the Hong Kong umbrella movement. *Journal of Creative Communications, 13*(2), 157–165.
Wueest, B., Rothenhäusler, K., & Hutter, S. (2013). Using computational linguistics to enhance protest event analysis. *ENCoRe workshop 'Tools and techniques for conflict event data collection'*.
Yeung, T. K., Pang, K. L., Leung, M. K., & Leung, C. S. (2020). *Uncontrollable violence, backed by Beijing: Who can exercise checks and balances on Hong Kong police*. Spring Hill Publishing.
Yu, M. (2015). *Framing occupy central: A content analysis of Hong Kong, American and British newspaper coverage*. University of South Florida, Graduate Theses and Dissertations.
Yuen, W. W. T., & Mok, F. K. T. (2014). Promoting national identification through civic education: A study of the views of civic educators in Hong Kong. *Citizenship, Social and Economics Education, 13*(2), 82–92.
Yule, G. (1996). *Pragmatics*. Oxford University Press.

GPSR Compliance
The European Union's (EU) General Product Safety Regulation (GPSR) is a set of rules that requires consumer products to be safe and our obligations to ensure this.

If you have any concerns about our products, you can contact us on

ProductSafety@springernature.com

In case Publisher is established outside the EU, the EU authorized representative is:

Springer Nature Customer Service Center GmbH
Europaplatz 3
69115 Heidelberg, Germany

www.ingramcontent.com/pod-product-compliance
Ingram Content Group UK Ltd.
Pitfield, Milton Keynes, MK11 3LW, UK
UKHW020704041026
15590UKWH00001B/454
* 9 7 8 3 0 3 1 2 7 5 8 3 8 *